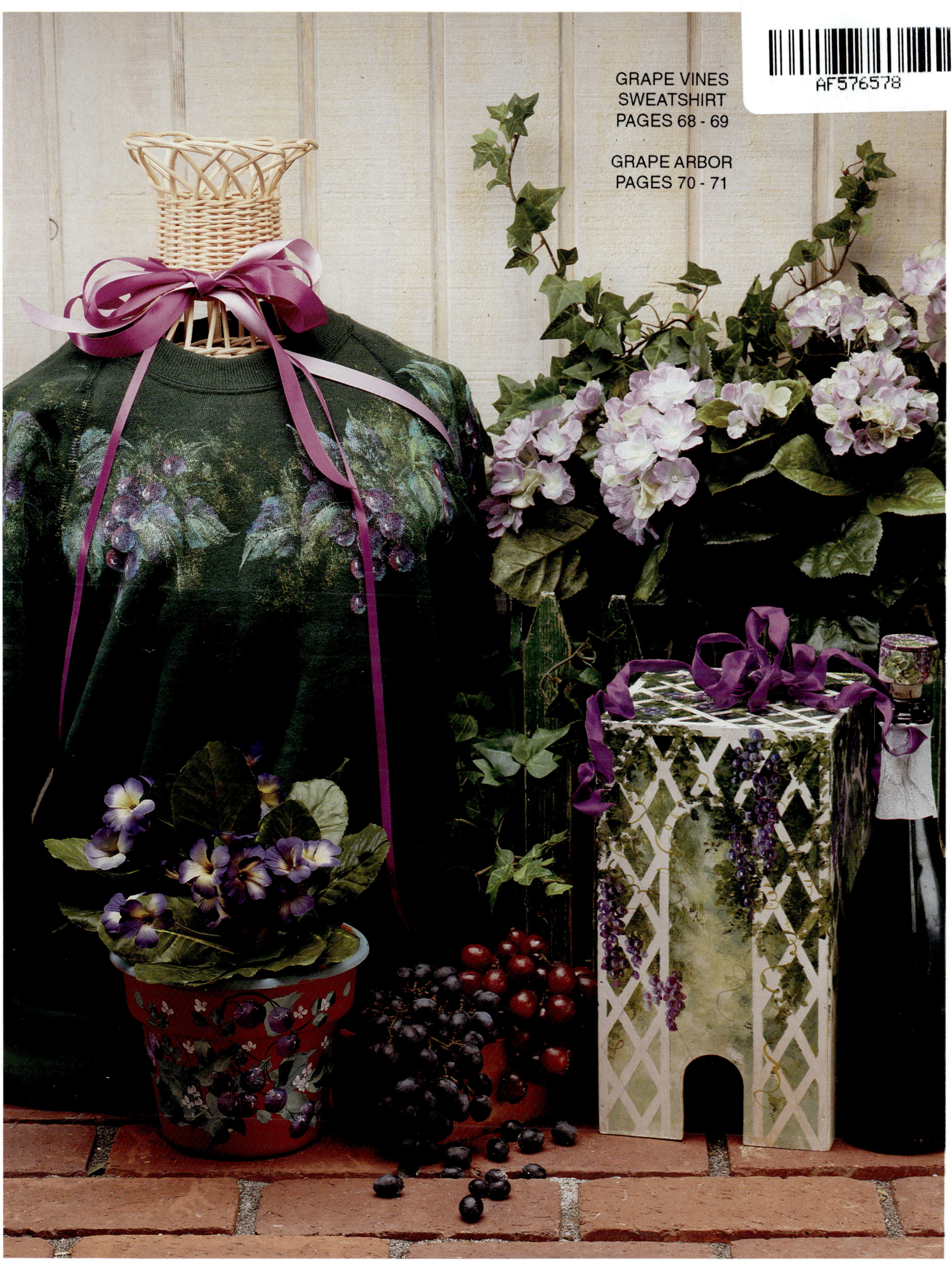
GRAPE VINES
SWEATSHIRT
PAGES 68 - 69
GRAPE ARBOR
PAGES 70 - 71

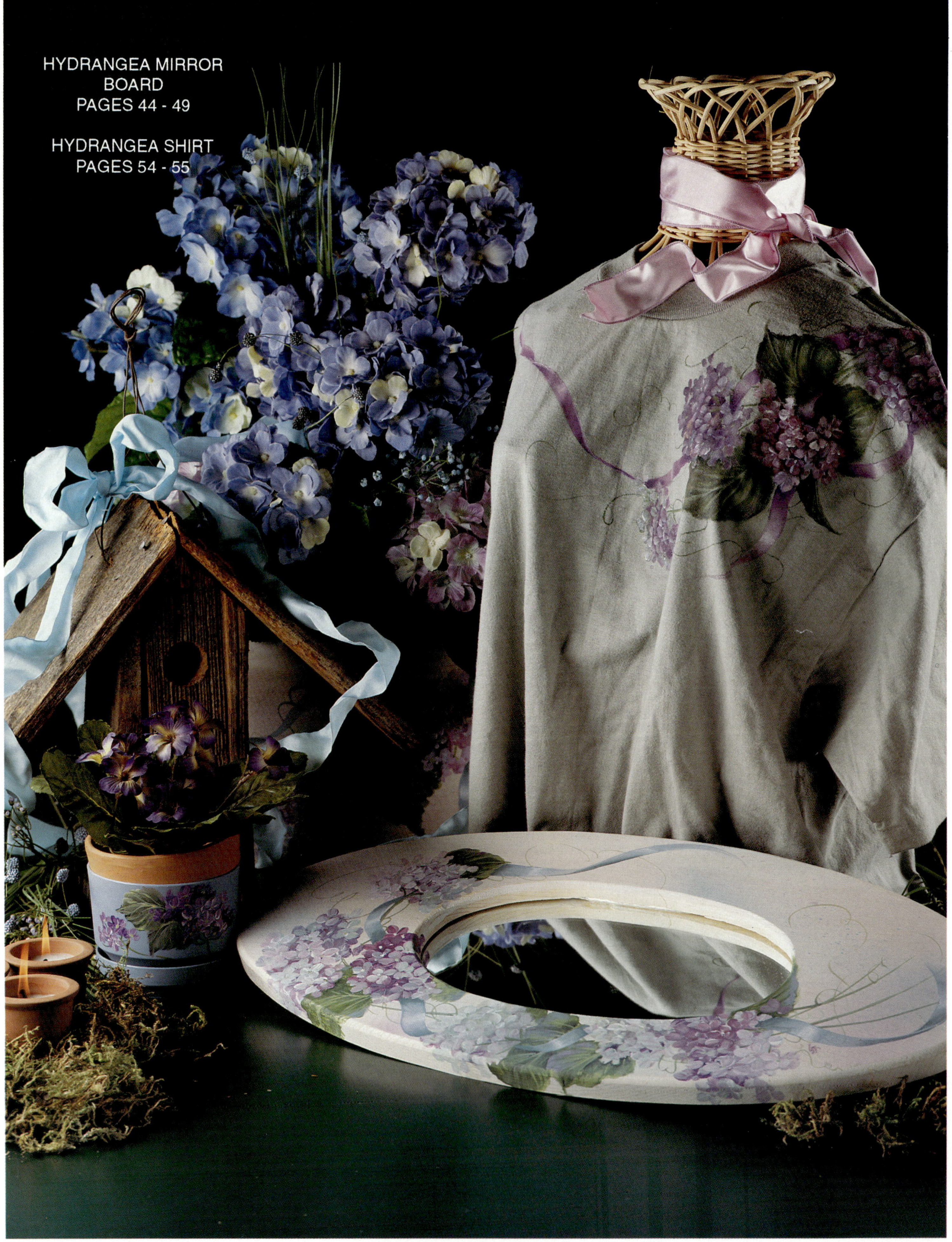
HYDRANGEA MIRROR
BOARD
PAGES 44 - 49

HYDRANGEA SHIRT
PAGES 54 - 55

Introduction

When I was a little girl we lived with my grandmother. She loved her garden and we always had fresh flowers or greens in vases or baskets throughout the house. At the holidays we would all gather, cut and clip branches, fruit, berries and foliage to decorate every corner inside and out. The smell was wonderful.

Now that I get to be Gran I want to make memories too. Gran's House is full of beautiful blossoms, boughs, berries, and bright ribbons. Gather these to decorate your home from top to bottom. Paint on walls, cabinets, doors, linens, and any treasures you find. Finish with lots of love and laughter.

I hope you will paint wonderful pieces that will be heirlooms for generations to come. Paint with a loving heart and come often to Gran's House to visit me and my angel babies.

Ros Stallcup
1436 Lakeview Drive
Virginia Beach, Va. 23455
804-464-4974

Painted Pieces may be ordered from;

Gran's Garden
3961 Rainbow Drive
Virginia Beach, VA 23462
804-471-5002 Fax 804-464-4185

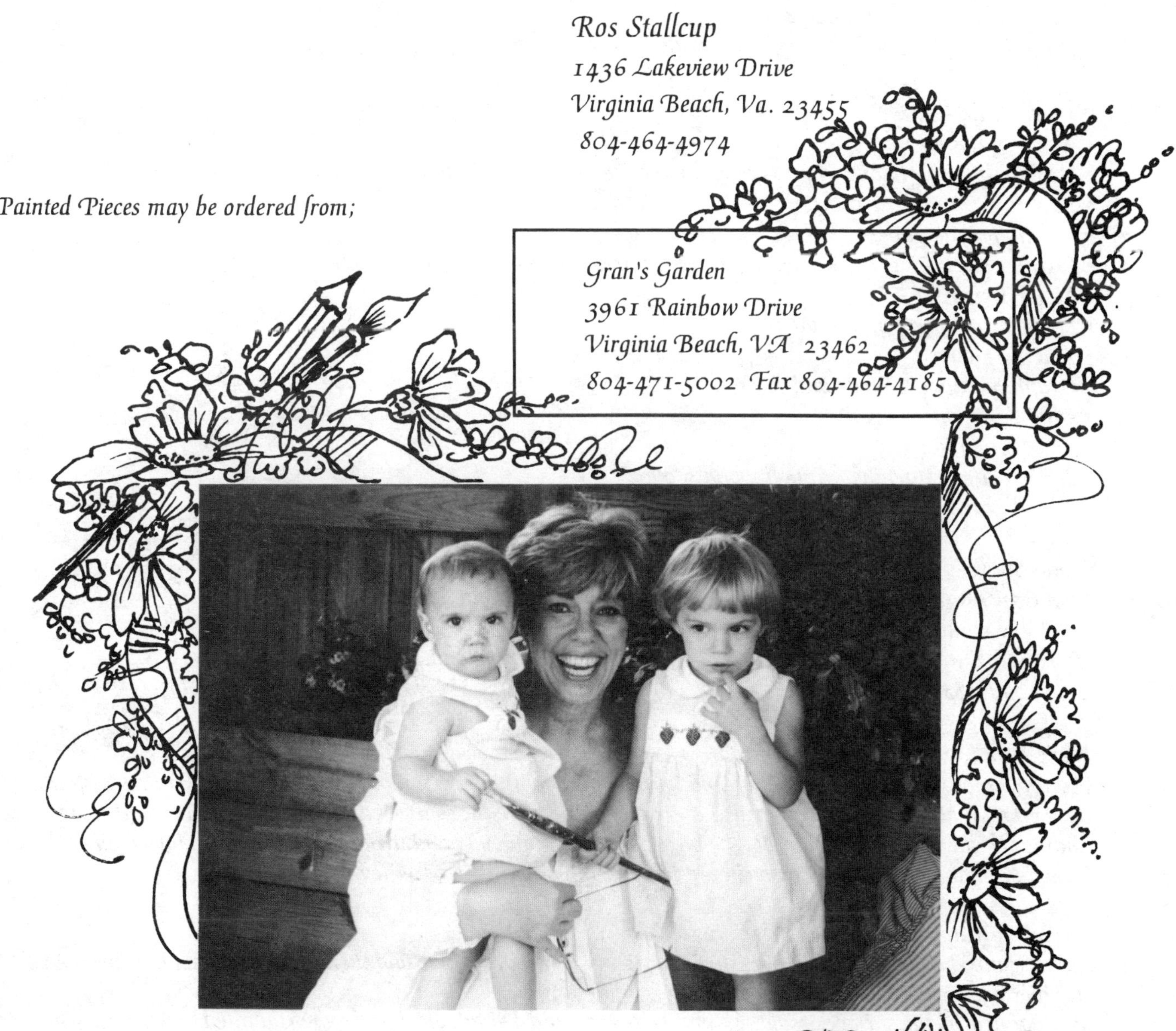

Supplies

All supplies can be purchased at your local art and craft stores, some are found in hardware stores. If you have difficulty finding something contact Susan Scheewe Publications or if you have a retail shop, Stan Brown's Arts and Crafts. Other sources will be noted on special items.

Paints - Listed in each project

I have used DecoArt Americana Acrylic Paints, Ultra Gloss Acrylic Enamel, and So Soft Fabric Acrylic. Always refer to the color pictures. There are many variations of color. Consider Red, as an example. Anything close to the color red will work. It doesn't have to be exactly the same shade of red. Make your own color charts. Put the color samples alphabetically in an inexpensive address book.

Brushes

I used Scheewe Martin/F. Weber brushes and Stan Brown's brushes. The foliage brush is a hog bristle brush cut on an angle. All other brushes are soft synthetic hair.

Flats - 1/4 inch , 1/2 inch
Round - # 2 and 5
Liner - # 1 and 10 x 0
Angular Shader 1/4", 3/8' and 1/2" Scheewe Angular Shader S8008 Martin/F. Weber
Filbert (Cat's Tongue) - # 2, 4 and 8
Suzie's Foliage Brush - 3/4" Scheewe Foliage Angular S8037 Martin/F. Weber

General Supplies

- *Water container*
- *Masking tape 1/4" and wider (3M recommended - found in Automotive paint store)*
- *Tack rag*
- *Acrylic palette paper*
- *Pigma Pens (.05 extra fine point permanent marker). Recommended.*
- *Paper Towels*
- *Stylus or a red ink ball-point pen*
- *Tracing paper*
- *Graphite Paper - White and Gray*
- *#400 Sandpaper*
- *J.W. Wood filler*
- *J. W. White Lightening or other wood sealer*
- *J.W. Right Step waterbased varnish*

Wood Sources

Stan Brown's Arts and Craft
13435 E. Whitaker Wa y
Portland, OR 97230
1-800 547-5531

Susan Scheewe Publications
13435 N E Whitaker Way
Portland, OR 97230
503-254-9100 Fax 503-252-9508

Basic Wood Preparation.

Fill any holes with J.W. Wood Filler and let them dry completely. Sand level. I have used White Lightning as a base coat on all my pieces as it is also a great sealer. Leave the white-washed effect of White Lightning or add another coat with acrylic color. Let the base coat dry completely and then sand lightly with fine sand paper or a brown paper bag. The final finish should feel smooth but not slick to the touch.

Tin or Galvanized Metal

Surface must be clean and free of rust. Sand lightly to rough surface and then spray with metal primer. Allow to dry and paint with two coats of acrylic.

Pre-painted metal surfaces, such as mailboxes, should be sanded lightly then painted. Varnish when dry. Exterior Spar Varnish is great on dark colors but will yellow over time. On white backgrounds I have used two coats of water base varnish. For outside pieces re-varnish as necessary to protect them.

Transferring Patterns on Wood or Other Firm Surface.
Trace pattern on to tracing paper. Position the tracing paper pattern on surface and anchor in place using masking tape. Place graphite paper underneath the tracing paper pattern with dark side down. Transfer basic lines by retracing the pattern using a stylist or ball point pen. I like to use a red ball point pen so I can see which lines I have traced. Always check as you get started to see that the lines are transferring properly. Take your time; a clear, crisp pattern is worth the extra few minutes.

Transferring Patterns to Soft Fabric or Sweat Shirt.
Trace pattern onto tulle (a fine nylon netting) using a permanent marking pen. Position tulle tracing on the fabric or sweat shirt and again hold in place with masking tape. In the case of wearable art it is always wise to check placement of design by trying it on and looking in a mirror. Retrace the design through the tulle using a charcoal pencil, white or black, depending on the color of your fabric.

Definitions

Basecoat - To apply the first layer of color.

Shading and Highlighting - To apply color on top of the base coat, both dark and light, to give dimension to your painting.

Detailing - To add fine lines, flower centers, stems, and other touches to give a finished look to your painting.

Tapping - To tap very lightly using the tip of the brush, bouncing around rather than moving in straight rows. Use this technique to create foliage or flowers.

Double Load Brush - Having two colors in your brush at the same time. First pick up the lighter color on one corner of the brush and stroke it on the palette. Then pick the other color on the opposite edge (corner) of the brush and stroke on the palette. The desired effect is the have pure color on each edge or corner of the brush and a gradual blending of the two colors in the middle of the brush.

Pick your Paint
***DecoArt Americana** paint is used on most of these projects. I have used Brush and Blend on some of these projects to achieve transparent effects and to aid in blending. If you prefer another brand of paints refer to an interchange chart.*

***DecoArt Ultra Gloss Acrylic Enamel** is great to use on slick surfaces such as glass, china, enamel wear dishes, and plastic. This paint is dishwasher safe when you bake your finished piece in your oven at 325 degrees for 30 minutes. Always read the manufactures label on the bottle.*

***DecoArt So Soft Fabric Acrylic**. These paints will penetrate the fabric and remain soft to the touch. The colors are clear and crisp. Use So Soft like watercolors by adding water or textile medium. Each fabric will take water and paint differently so experiment to find what works best for your project. So Soft Fabric Acrylic requires no heat setting and it is not necessary to use textile medium. Use a fabric board or non porous surface under your fabric as the paint may go through to the back. Always refer to the manufacture's label or fact sheets for complete information.*

Fabrics made of cotton and synthetic blends are best for painting as they tend not to fade or shrink. Smooth surface fabrics are easiest to pattern and paint..

Ready made napkins and placemats are great to paint. It is always best to wash fabric first to remove any sizing.

Helpful Hints

Painting is something you do alone, for yourself, so remember to have fun. Follow your own instincts about color and form. Don't be afraid to experiment with other colors as there are many colors found in our gardens. This book is only a guide to some techniques that may help you to accomplish these and other projects.

Many of the flowers in this book are the ones that grow in my garden. Try to paint the flowers that grow in your garden. Take time to smell and really look at the structure of a flower. I try to create the illusion of a flower with a few dabs of paint, and a hint of their structure, to give the effect.

Be patient with yourself. Practice will make a big difference. If you are not happy with what you have painted then just re-paint it! Rubbing alcohol removes areas of dry acrylic from sealed wood, or allow the paint to dry and simply paint over. Do it again, and again, until you are satisfied.

Painting Flowers

When painting either stroke flowers or tapped flowers squeeze out small amounts of your colors and get fresh paint often for the best results. I fill my brush full so that I can stroke and tap with a light touch to achieve a delicate look. Because I often have a lot of paint in my brush it is vital that you clean your brush often while you are painting. Cleaning will keep paint from drying up in the ferrule of your brushes and ruining that great shape that is helping you paint beautiful flowers.

If you are consistently unhappy with your results consider a new brush. Practice Practice Practice.

While you are painting keep your brushes in water and clean them out often and thoroughly before you put them aside. I have been using Deco Magic Brush & Hand Cleaner.

Lets begin

Practice the flowers on tracing paper first.

Paint background foliage first and let it dry. Pattern on top if you feel more secure, but try free handing these flowers using your pattern as a guide for positioning. Paint main flowers next, add leaves, filler flowers and stem and squiggles. Put these flowers together as it pleases you. Remember you are painting your own gardens.

Daisies

Use either a round or filbert brush. Brush size will vary according to the size of your petals. Most of my daises are painted with a #4 or #6 filbert brush.

Load your brush by pulling through the puddle of Titanium White several times. Start your daisy with the center, touching down with the side of the brush to form an oval. Pull each petal as in the illustration starting with the tip of the brush, handle straight up. Push down on the brush and pull toward the center, lifting as you pull. Vary the length of your petals. Petals #1 and #2 are the longest. Complete all your daisies, add calyxes and stems using one of your shades of green. Paint centers with Cadmium Yellow. Shade lower section with Burnt Sienna. three and four petal flower clusters on top with Cherry Red and then with Cadmium Orange.

Practice Practice Practice

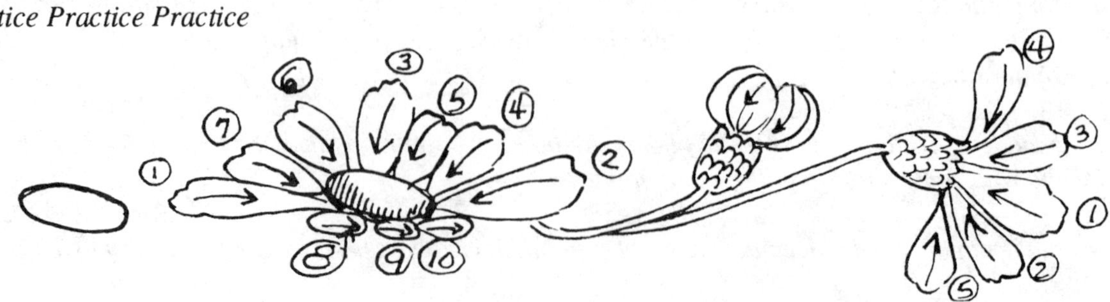

Berries

Paint these berries with a Q-Tip. Sue Scheewe taught me this technique years ago and I have had more fun painting these berries. It works great for blackberries, raspberries, holly berries, small grapes, pyracantha berries, and bittersweet. Let your imitation work for you. For smaller berries pull some of cotton off the end of your Q-Tip.(inexpensive cotton swabs work great as they have less cotton the tip.) Moisten and roll the tip in your fingers to reshape it before taping in the paint. To create large berries try tapping in to paint with wooden dowels of various sizes . Be generous with your paint and tap into various colors at one time .

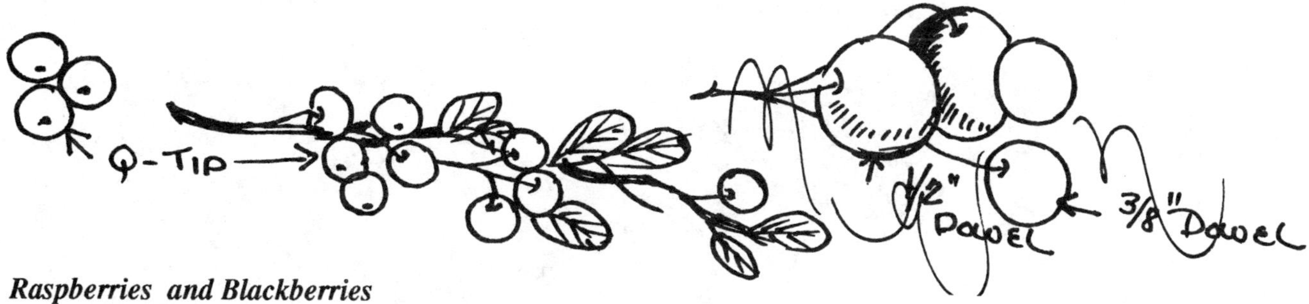

Raspberries and Blackberries

Touch the tip of Q-Tip one time into Dioxazine Purple, touch once or twice on your palette with the tip until a circle with a hole in the center forms. Have plenty of paint on your Q-Tip and touch lightly. Paint one half the berry with Dioxazine Purple then touch the dirty tip of Q-Tip into Red Violet and tap the other half of the berry. Highlight on the Red Violet side by touching into Titanium White (always tap on your palette a few times when picking up fresh paint). Do all your berries at the same time. Vary the colors and sizes. Unripe berries have touches of Titanium White and Olive Green. Paint stems and little green leaves with a small brush using one of your shades of green. Pick a shade that will show against your background. Highlight on the light side of half of the berries with Titanium White and paint a little curved line for a shine using a No. 10x0 liner brush.

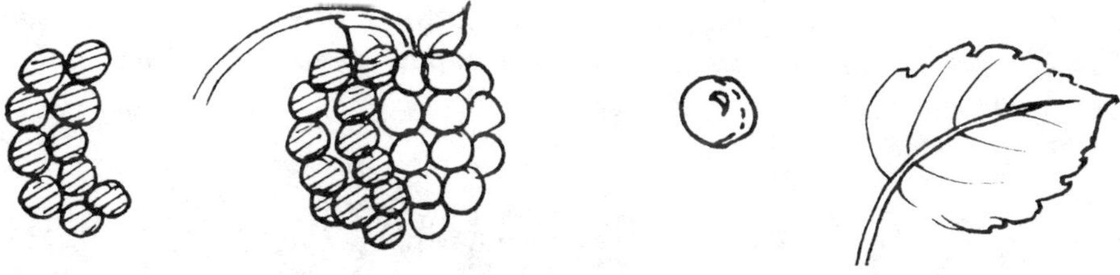

Hydrangea

Hydrangea blossoms are large ball shaped flowers composed of clusters of four petal blossoms. The colors range from blue to pink to purple. In the fall they turn pink to gray green with tints of mauve and they dry beautifully.

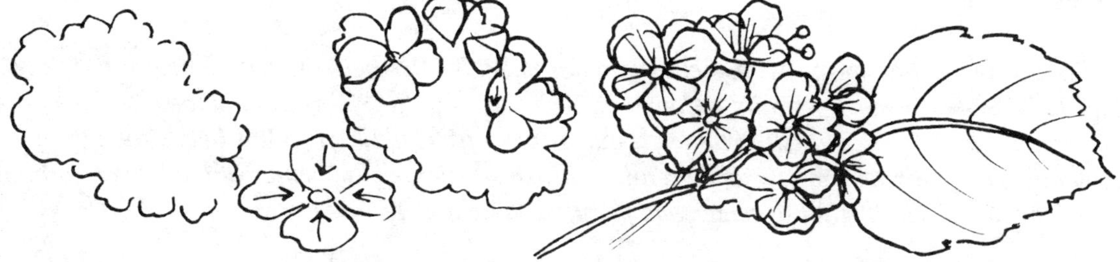

I painted them with a filbert brush, size will be determined by the size of the blooms. Colors will be determined by the shades you want to achieve. Start with a cluster of dabs of the darkest value paint. Pick up Titanium White with some of your base color and create three and four petal blossoms on top of base color. Extend over the edges and place flowers at different angles. As you create the clusters of flowers vary colors by picking up pinks, lavenders, and blues. Add stems and large leaves with shades of green. Notice that the

Hydrangea (continued)

large ball shapes are seen at different angles and some seen from the side look like ovals. New blossoms are light green and are painted to look like little dots with a few four petal flowers.

Geraniums

Geraniums are painted like Hydrangeas only not as dense a cluster of blossoms so that some stems can show through. Base the cluster with a color such as Napa Red allow to dry. Paint three four petal flower clusters on top with Cherry Red and then with Cadmium Orange.

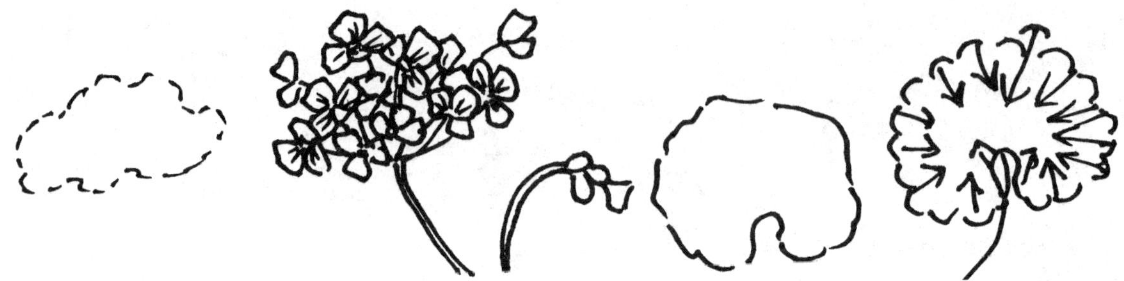

Geranium leaves are slightly ruffled and round. Base with Avocado and shade with Evergreen. Flip overlapping strokes from the edges of the leaf using a filbert brush and Olive Green creating slight ruffles. Paint stems and squiggles with 10x0 liner brush and a shade of green picked to show best with your background color.

Lilacs

Lilacs are clusters of blossoms and have heart shaped leaves. Paint these flowers with a small filbert brush size 2 or 4. Tap loose spiky shape of Dioxazine Purple then pick up Titanium White, Lavender, Baby Blue, and Dioxazine purple as you create three and four petal flowers. Paint unopened blossoms on the tips with little dots of colors. Create little stems with olive green and No.10x0 liner. These flowers make great filler or "tappy flowers" that can be added to any design.

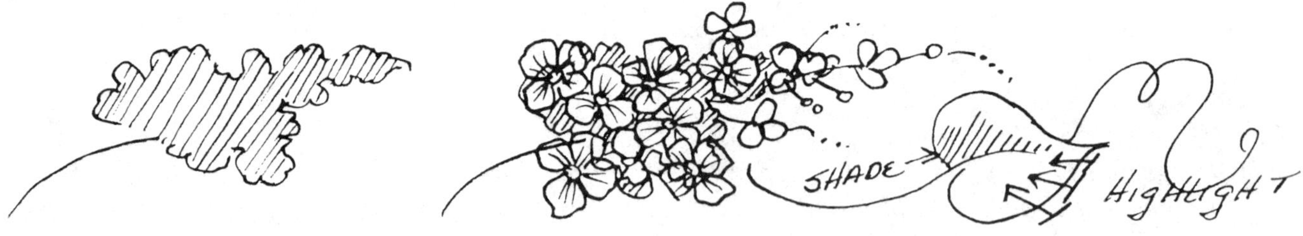

Daffodils

Daffodils always signal spring with their sunny faces. Paint the bell shaped center of the flowers first with Antique Gold and allow to dry. Paint a Cadmium Yellow oval of little dots around the top of the flower using the tip of a small round or liner brush. Paint vertical stripes with Cadmium Yellow below the dots to create ridges. Paint petals with Cadmium Yellow using a filbert brush starting at the center of the flower and pulling toward the tip of the petal. Highlight the center and petals with Lemon Yellow.

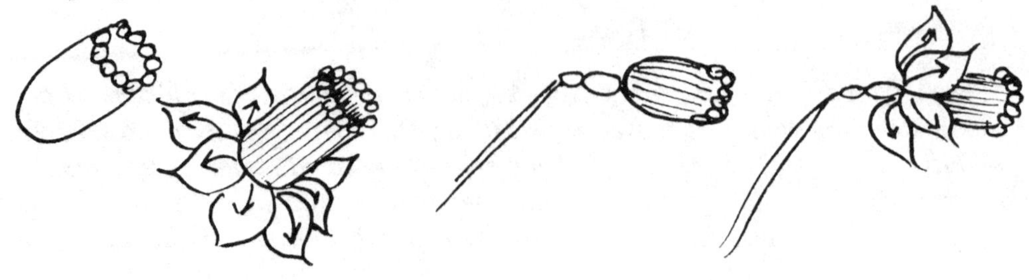

Strawberries

Paint base coat of Calico Red on all strawberries using an angle shader brush (size determined by the size of your berries). Shade the dark side by tipping the point of your angle shader into Calico Red and Dioxazine Purple, pull brush strokes on your palette to mix colors in brush. Highlight on the light side with Cadmium Orange and Titanium White. Paint Titanium White highlight in center of berry blending while still wet into base color. If necessary help the colors blend by picking up some Calico red. Paint cross hatch lines over the lightest area with Titanium White using your 10x0 liner brush. Paint seeds with Black and Cadmium Yellow in and around the cross hatched lines using your No. 10x0 liner brush.

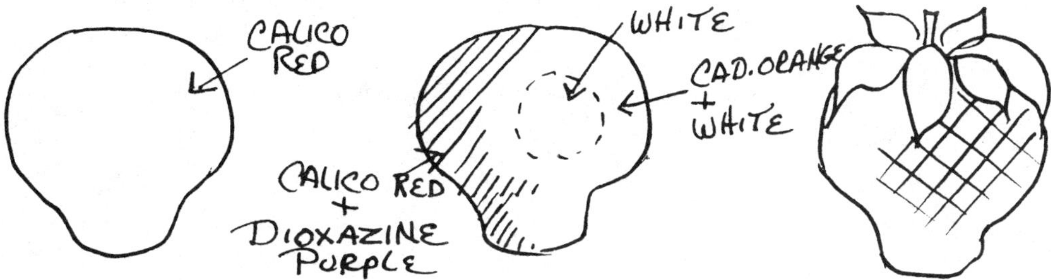

Wisteria

Wisteria blossoms are hanging cluster of pale lavender blossom that grow on vines. Paint the blossoms with Dioxazine Purple and Titanium White using a No. 2 filbert brush. Pull littlestrokes using the side edge of your brush from bottom of the blossom to the top, forming little hanging clusters. Leaves are painted with Avocado Green using a small filbert brush. See illustration for structure. Paint vine and tendrils with Avocado Green using your No 10x0 liner brush.

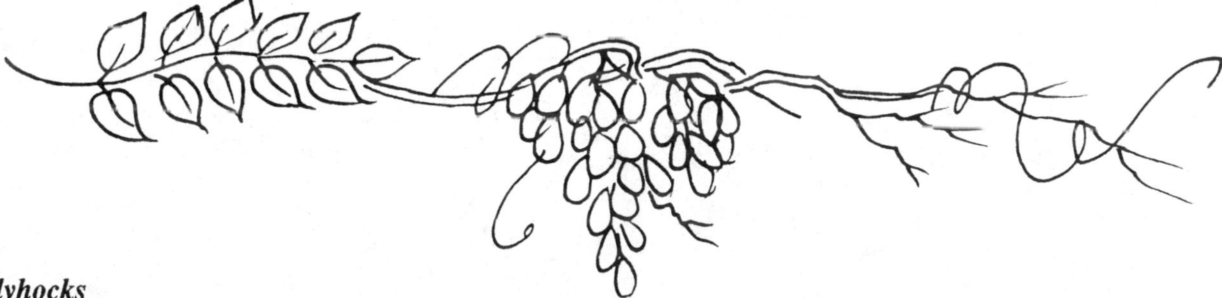

Hollyhocks

Hollyhocks are tall spiky flowers. Start by painting ovals with Burgundy Wine using your No. 4 round brush. Create flowers by painting oval shapes with White and Baby Pink on top of some of the Burgundy Wine shapes. Turn flowers in different directions and add a few dots to create tips of flowers. Tuck little leaves at random in and around the flowers using the tip of your round brush and Avocado. Paint stems with Olive Green using No. 10x0 liner brush.

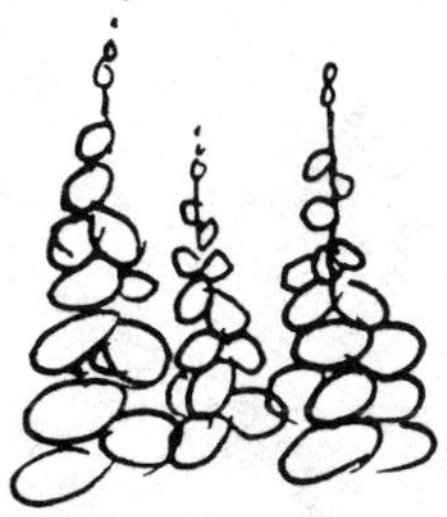
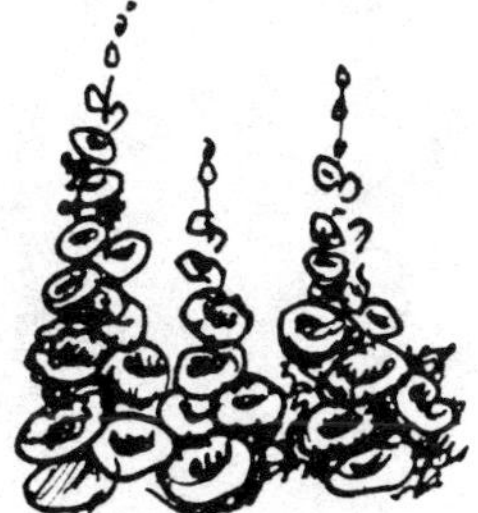
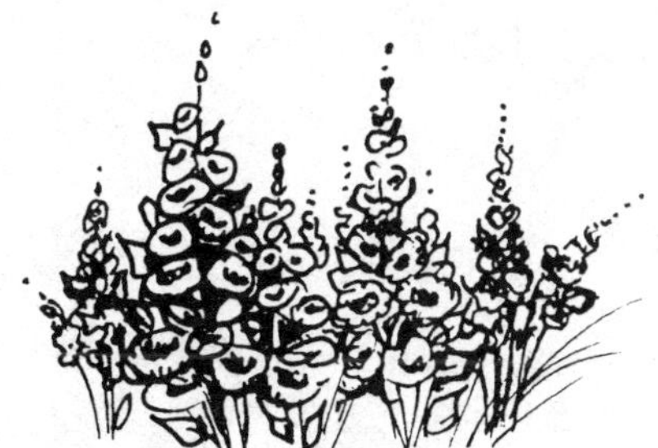

Squishy Leaves

These leaves are called squishy leaves because you create them by squishing the paint from underneath your brush. Paint squishy leaves with any combination of shades of green using a flat brush. Remember you must have a generous amount of paint in your brush for it to squish to form this leaf. Pull brush through fresh paint, turn brush and pull again, tip one edge into an other shade of green. Paint leaf by pushing the flat of the brush sideways across the surface, lift up to the chisel edge of the brush in the center of the leaf and slip forward to make a slight point. Practice Practice Practice. I usually paint three of the leaves together and add a stem with a liner brush.

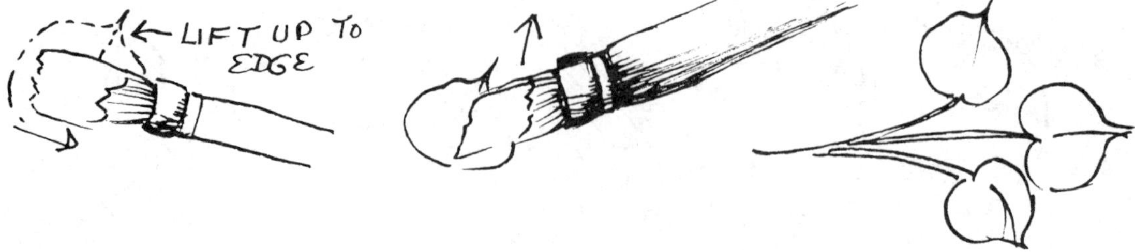

Stems and Squiggles

Paint stems and squiggles with your liner brush. Pick up your paint with a little water, pull your brush through the paint a few times to load it fully with this wet mixture. Balance your brush hand on your other hand. The handle of the brush should be pointing straight up. Touch only the tip of the brush to the surface.

Pull the tip of the brush toward you applying as little pressure as possible. This will create a narrow fluid line like ink from a pen. Practice swirling the brush by stiffening your wrist and moving your entire arm to form squiggles.

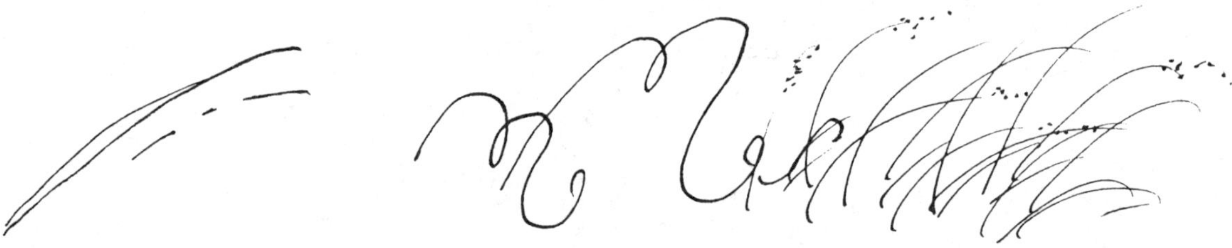

Foliage and Trees

Tap foliage with Suzie's Foliage Brush (3/4 inch Scheewe Foliage Brush No. S8037 Martin F. Weber) and any of your shades of green. Set brush in water before using to let the hairs of the brush fluff out.. Tap bristles on your palette to open hairs. Tip front half of the hairs into fresh paint and tap lightly on your palette. The point of the brush is up and tip the handle forward to use only the forward hairs. Tap gently on the surface to create foliage, many light taps are best, turning the brush in different directions.

Paint tree trunks with Mississippi Mud and a little water, using your No. 1 Liner Brush. Start with the trunk and lift up to form branches.

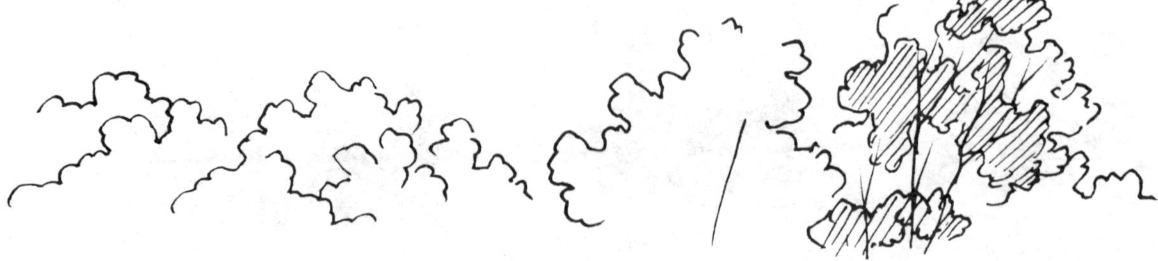

Petunias

Petunias are trumpet or bell shaped flowers, they can be many colors so have fun trying different combinations. Start with a base color using a filbert brush. The size of the brush is determined by the size of your flower. Highlight the edges of the petals with a lighter color using a lifting stroke back from the edges. Highlight one side of the base of the flower by pulling strokes with the edge of your brush. Add calyxes and stems with a green to contrast with your background. Leaves are heart shaped. Base leaves with Avocado. Shade with Evergreen on one side of the center vein. Highlight the leaves with Olive Green.

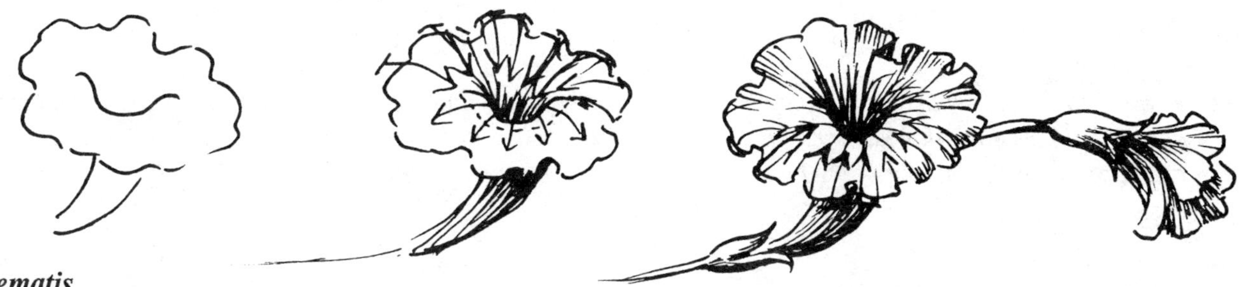

Clematis

Clematis come in many colors and sizes, pick a base color that you would want to grow in your garden. Paint base color on one flower at a time using a filbert brush. Pull overlapping stokes to form a three or four petal flower. Overstroke each petal with a lighter value (base color + white). Paint the flower centers with Avocado using a No. 6 round brush. Paint small lines and dots around the center with Cadmium Yellow using your liner brush.

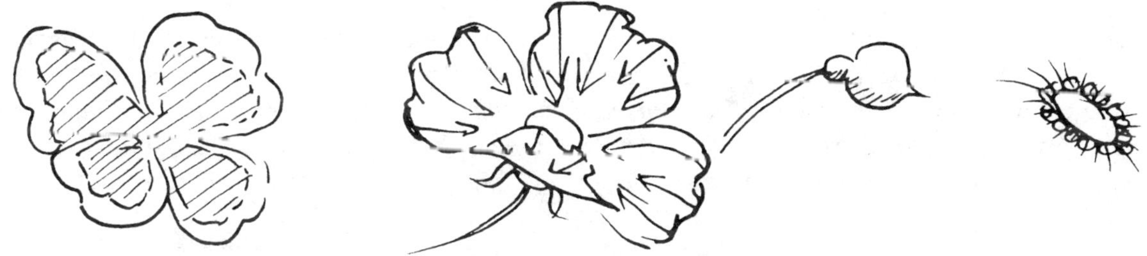

Poppies

Paint flowers with dark red base color using an angle shader. Highlight flowers with shades of Pink and Orange and white using a filbert brush. Paint centers with Avocado and Cadmium Yellow using a small round brush. Shade around centers and add little lines and dots with Dioxazine Purple.

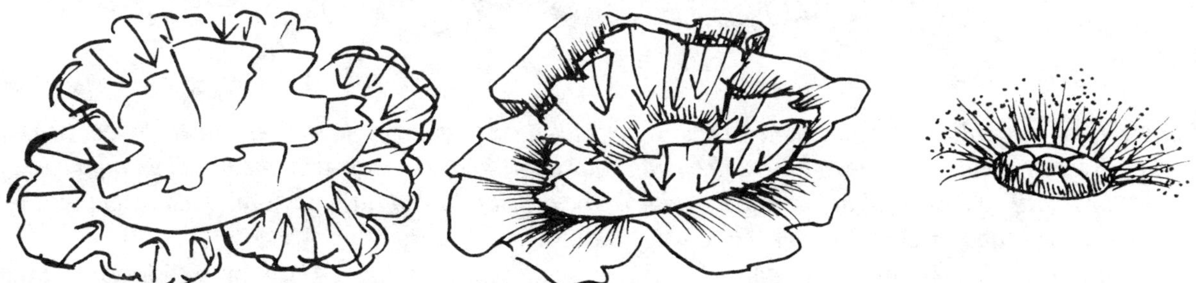

Grapes

Paint grapes as ovals with Dioxazine Purple, Burgundy Wine and Lavender using a filbert brush. Shade on the right side with Dioxazine Purple, True Blue and Baby Blue using your angle shader. Size of your brush is determined by the size of your grapes. Highlight with Orchid, Lavender and Titanium White. Let your colors vary as you paint the bunches of grapes. Paint Titanium White highlight.

Grapes (Continued)

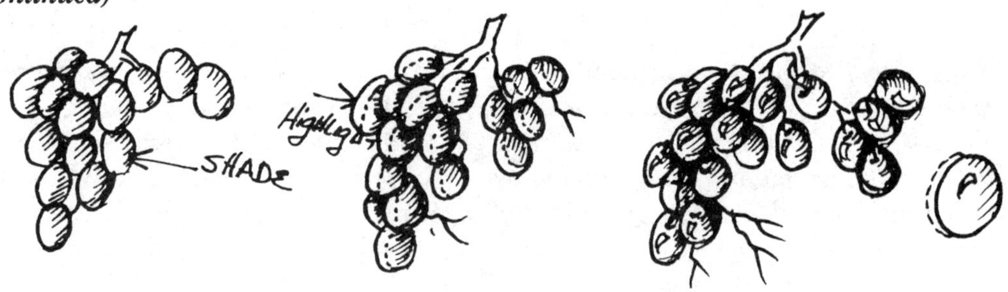

Rose Buds

Paint oval of base color with angle shader brush. Pick up lighter value on the tip of your dirty brush and stroke across the top edge of the flower. Pick up fresh paint on the tip of you brush and stroke across the lower front edge overlapping in the middle of the bud. Paint calyx and stem with green using your liner brush.

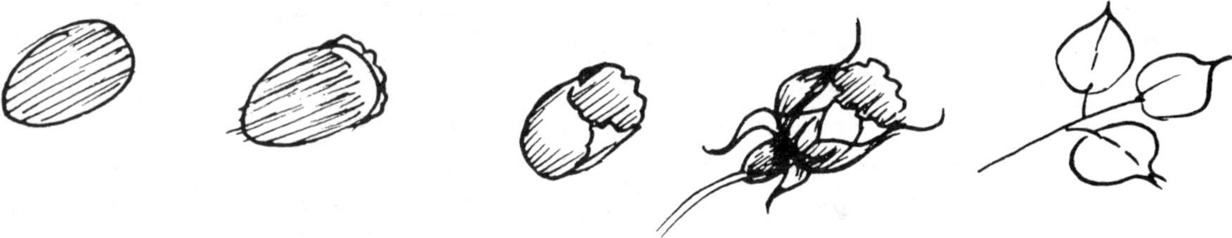

Poinsettias

Leaves and petals of Poinsettias are the same basic shape. I painted them like loose narrow triangles using an angle shader. Start up on the chisel edge of the brush, apply pressure and lift back up the chisel edge. These petals are loosely painted and can be done with more that one stroke. Paint some petals with Napa Red. allow to dry and add petals with Cherry Red and Cadmium Orange. Paint veins with a 10 x 0 liner and Napa Red. Centers are dots with Cadmium Yellow using the end of a paint brush or stylist. Paint red dot in the center of each yellow dot.

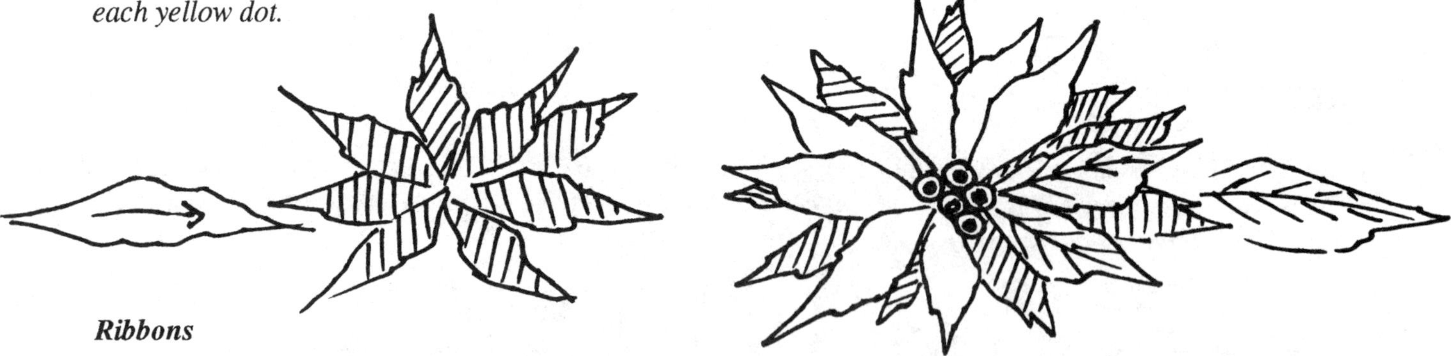

Ribbons

Paint ribbons any color to complement your design. I used a 3/8 inch angle shader brush. Select two values of a color. Base in ribbon with the lighter value using your angle shader. Start with the brush up on the edge, point up, pull and flatten brush. Lift back up to the edge of the brush pull and flatten again. This will make the ribbon look as if it turns and twists. Practice Practice Practice.

turn and position them many ways and I found it a great help in figuring out how they looked. Paint them different shades of green (dark, medium and light or any combination) using 1/2 inch angle shader brush. Vary the sizes and positions of leaves. Remember some leaves will be on top of each other. Cover one that displeases you with a new

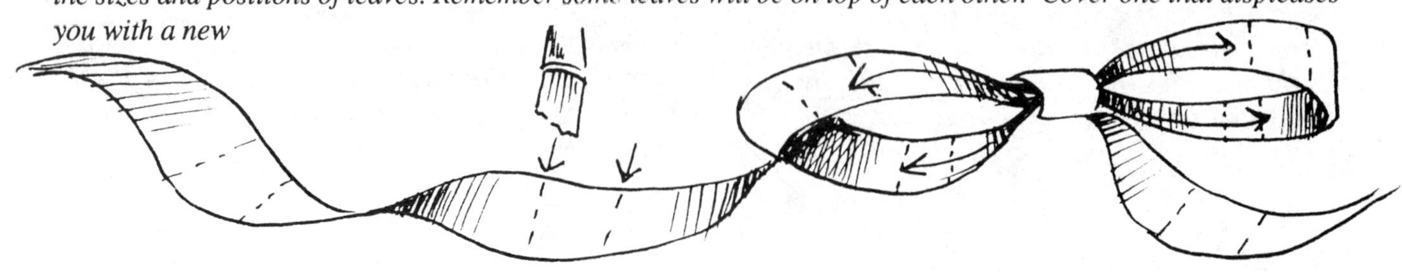

Ribbons (continued)

You can create simple bows and streamers using this same method. Pick up your paint by pulling the flat of the brush through fresh paint. Pick up your paint often so that it will flow as you pull your brush. Wipe stroke off with a damp paper towel if it gets away from you and do it again.

Highlight ribbon in widest places with double loaded brush with base color and white. Shade narrow places with double loaded brush with base color and dark value.

Ivy

As I started to paint ivy leaves, I pulled a few real leaves from my yard and placed them in front of me. I could turn and position them in many ways and I found it a great help in figuring out how they looked. Paint them different shades of green (dark, medium and light or any combination) using 1/2 inch angle shader brush. Vary the sizes and positions of leaves. Remember some leaves will be on top of each other. Cover one that displeases you with a new leaf.

Paint veins in all leaves with Olive Green (Olive Green with White in the lighest leaves) using No. 10 x 0 liner brush. Paint stems and squiggles with green to compliment your backyard.

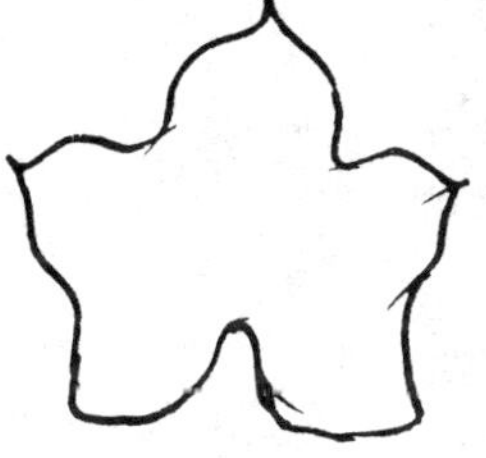
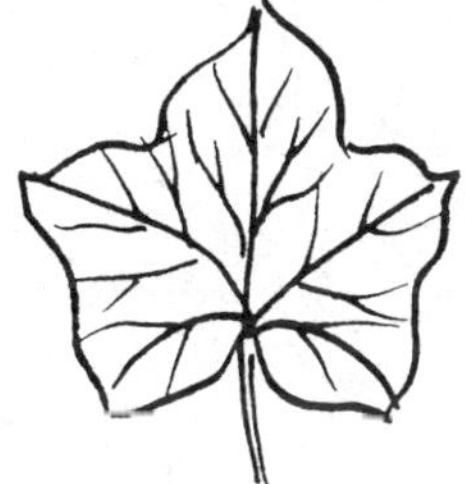
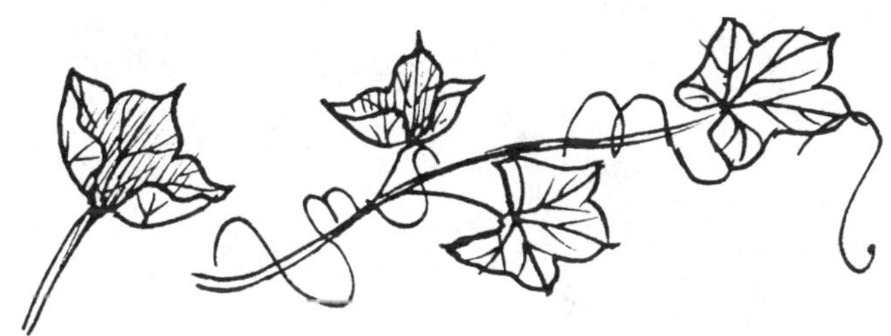

Basic Leaves

Basic leaves are a sloppy triangle shape. Base in leaves with Avocado using your angle shader. Darken one side of the center of each leaf with Evergreen using the point of your angle shader. Highlight

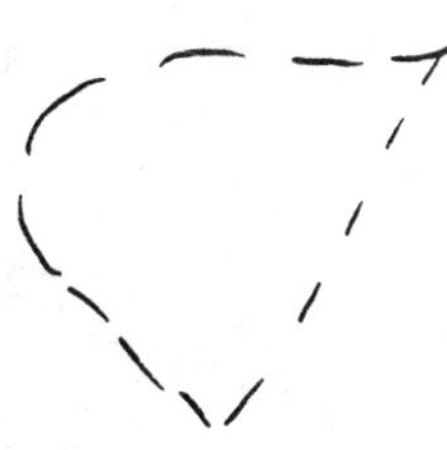
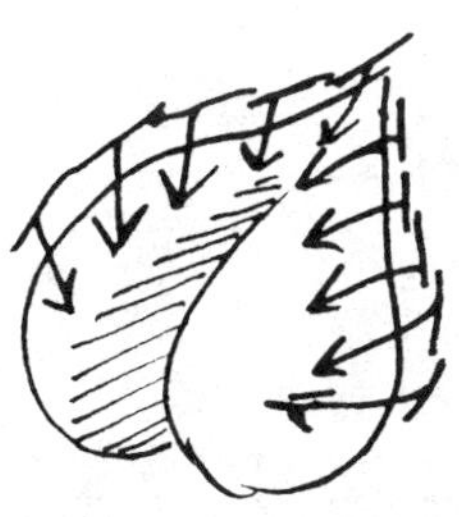
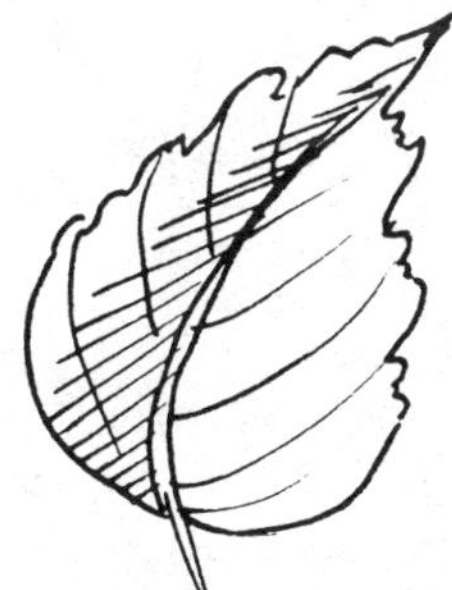

Holly Leaves

Transparent leave are painted with various shades of green using an angle shader. I touch the brush into Brush and Blend, blot on a paper towel then tip the point only into the paint. Using the brush flat leading with the point, paint the scalloped edge of the holly leaf on one side. Paint a curved line partly down the middle of the leaf. Now paint the opposite edge of the leaf. If opaque leaves are desired base leaves first with a middle value of green such as Avocado allow to dry then paint edges.

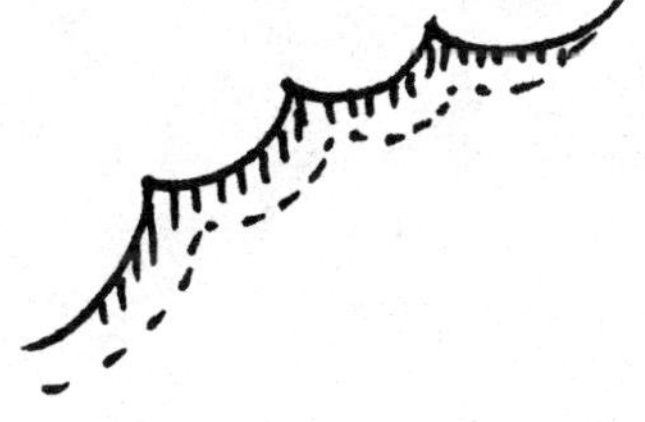
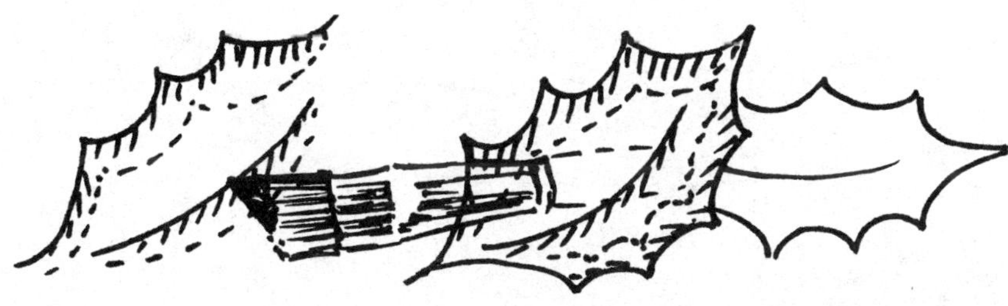

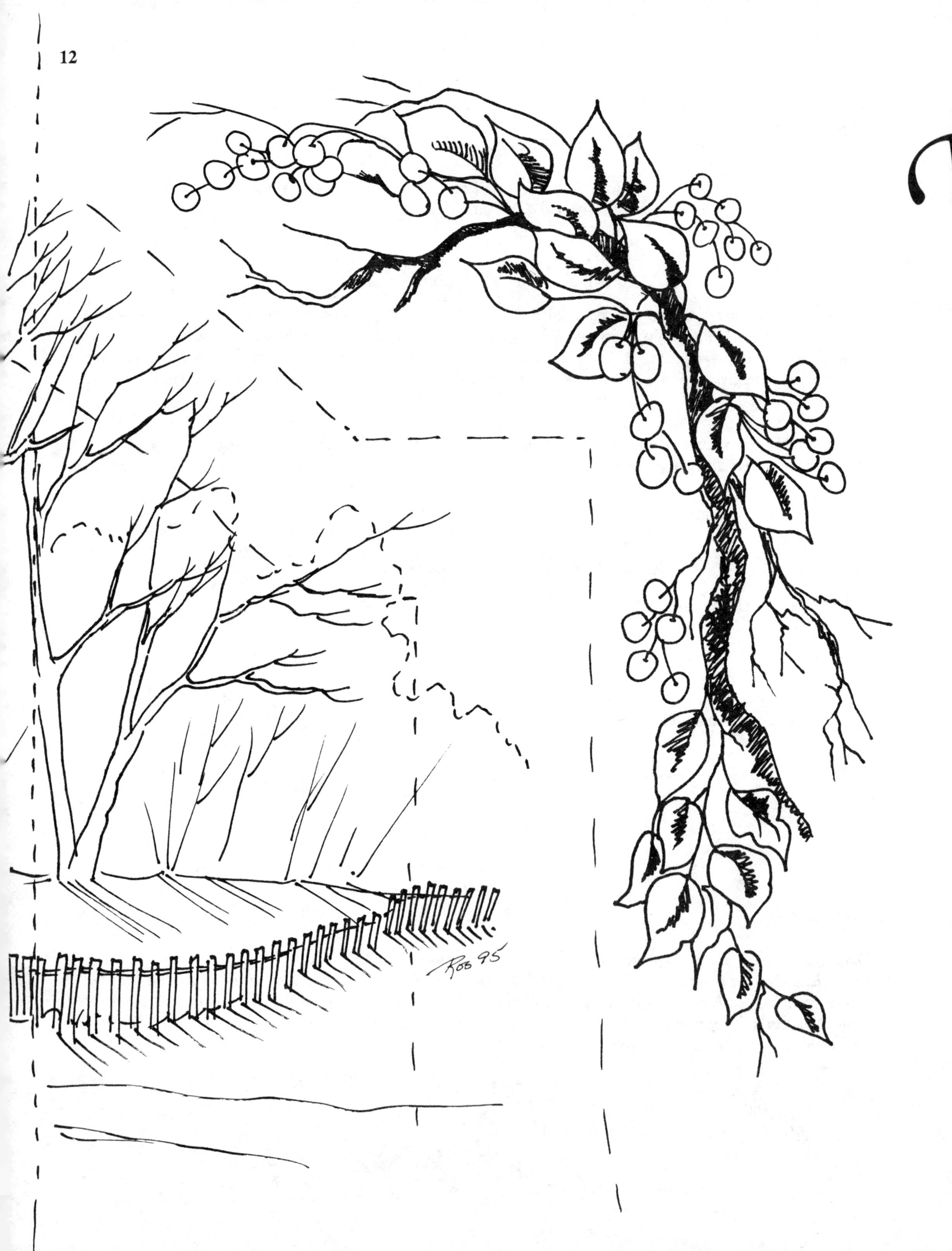
ROB 95

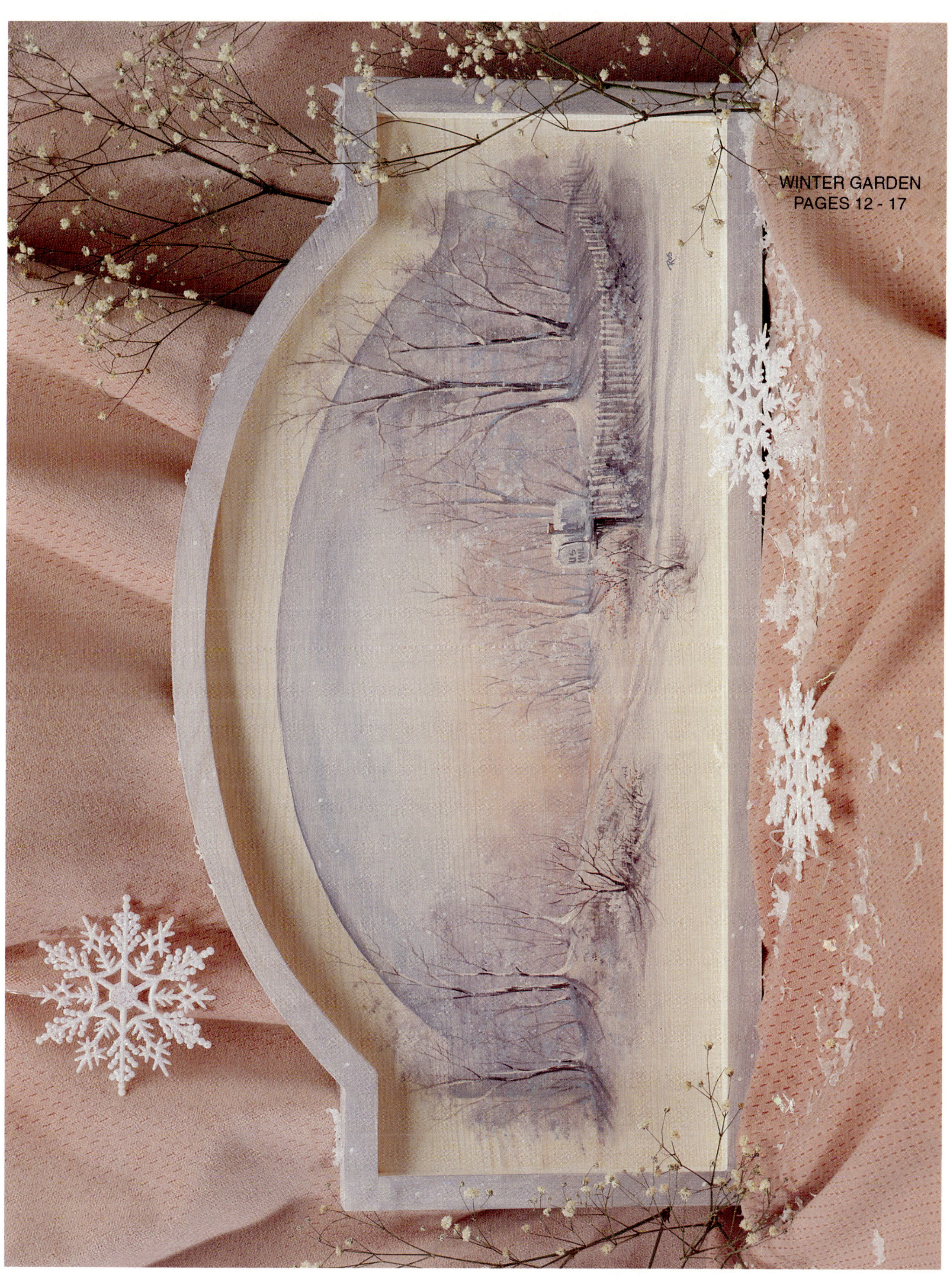

WINTER GARDEN
PAGES 12 - 17

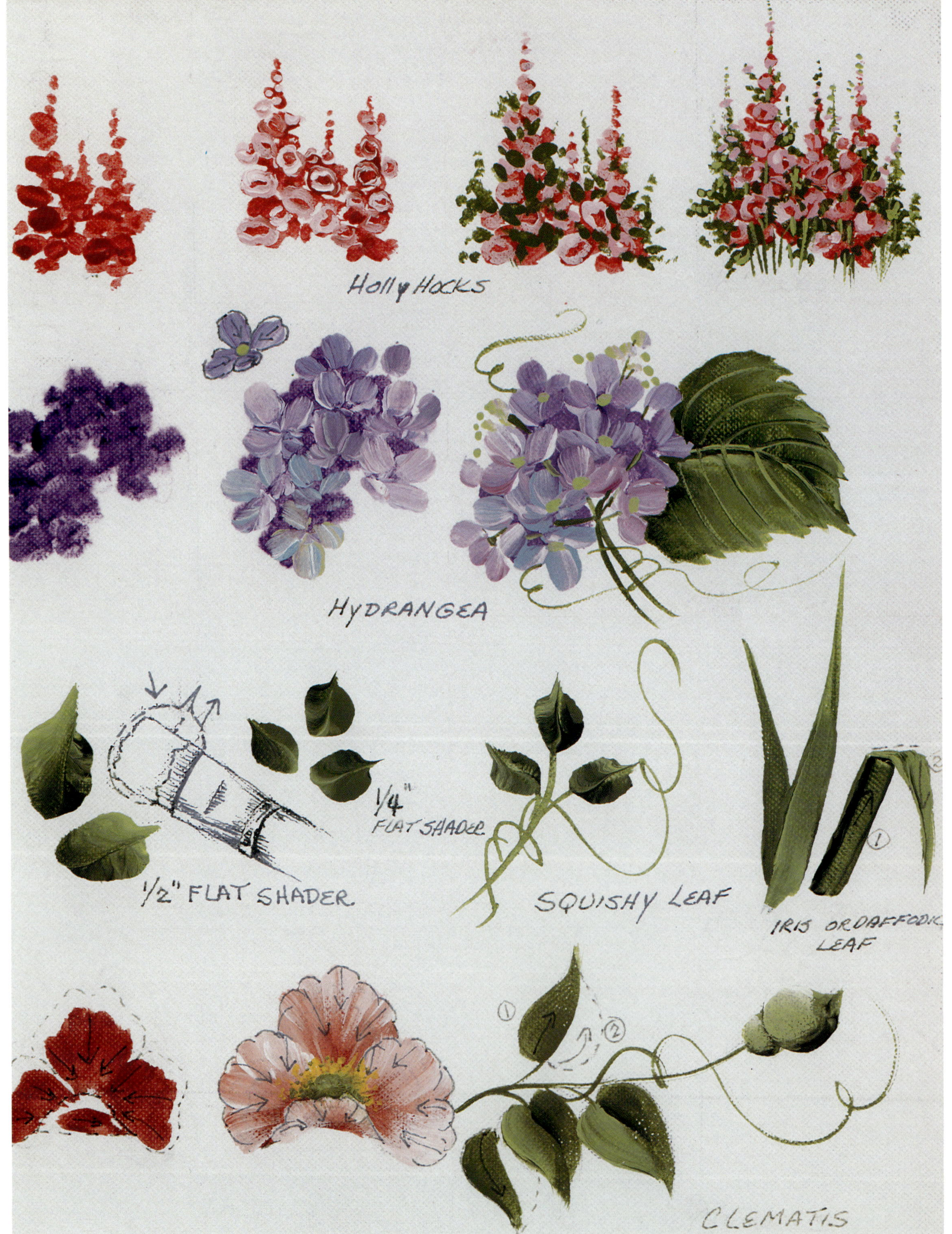
Holly Hocks
HYDRANGEA
1/4"
FLAT SHADER
1/2" FLAT SHADER
SQUISHY LEAF
IRIS OR DAFFODIL
LEAF
CLEMATIS

Winter Garden

Winter Garden

Surface: *Medium Goose Creek Sign Board - Stan Brown's Arts and Crafts*

Paints: *DecoArt Americana Acrylic*

Basecoat: *Paint board with White Lightning. Allow to dry and sand lightly.*

Transfer pattern: *Pattern upper shy line lightly with gray graphite if it is heavily marked erase with a soft eraser before you apply sky color. Pattern main tree trunks, ground lines and mailbox.*

Sky: *Paint Sky with Country Blue and a little Brush and Blend medium. Brushing across the sky as you work toward the horizon line lighten your color by picking up Hi Lite Flesh. Add a touch of Cadmium Orange at the horizon line to the left of center to create a bright sunset.. Allow to dry.*

Background Foliage: *Tap foliage using Suzie's Foliage Brush using Country Blue, Blue Mist, Hi-Lite Flesh and a little Plumb. Keep shapes light and air. This is just a suggestion of distant foliage.*

Tree Trunks: *Paint tree trunks using a liner brush and Paynes Gray, a touch of Cadmium Orange and Blue Mist. Highlight on the side of the tree facing the middle of the board with Hi-Lite Flesh. Add a touch of Cadmium Orange closest to the sunset.*

Snow Shadows: *Paint shadows with Country Blue and a touch of Plum. Brush lightly across and away from the sunset. Contour the land by slanting the brush slightly as you brush across.*

Tree Shadows and Fence: *Paint fence and shadows across the snow using a liner brush with Country Blue, Plum and a touch of Paynes Gray.*

Mailbox: *Base with Country Blue. Highlight front with Hi-Lite Flesh. Pile snow on top of the mailbox with Hi-Lite Flesh and a touch of Cadmium Orange. Paint " US Mail " with Paynes Gray and Titanium White.*

Bushes: *Tap bushes using the tip of the foliage Brush with Country Blue, plum, and Paynes Gray. Highlight bushes with Hi-lite Flesh and a touch of Cadmium Orange. Tap a few berries using the tip of a liner brush with Cadmium, Orange and Blue Mist.. Paint some long line grasses.*

Spatter: *Blue Mist and Hi-Lite Flesh.*

Edge of Board: *Paint the board edge with any of your colors and a little Brush and Blend. I used a pale wash of Country Blue.*

Winter Garden

*Paint "**Winter Garden**", "**Welcome**" or your family name on this board for a great gift. Transfer the letter with graphite and paint to match the boarder.*

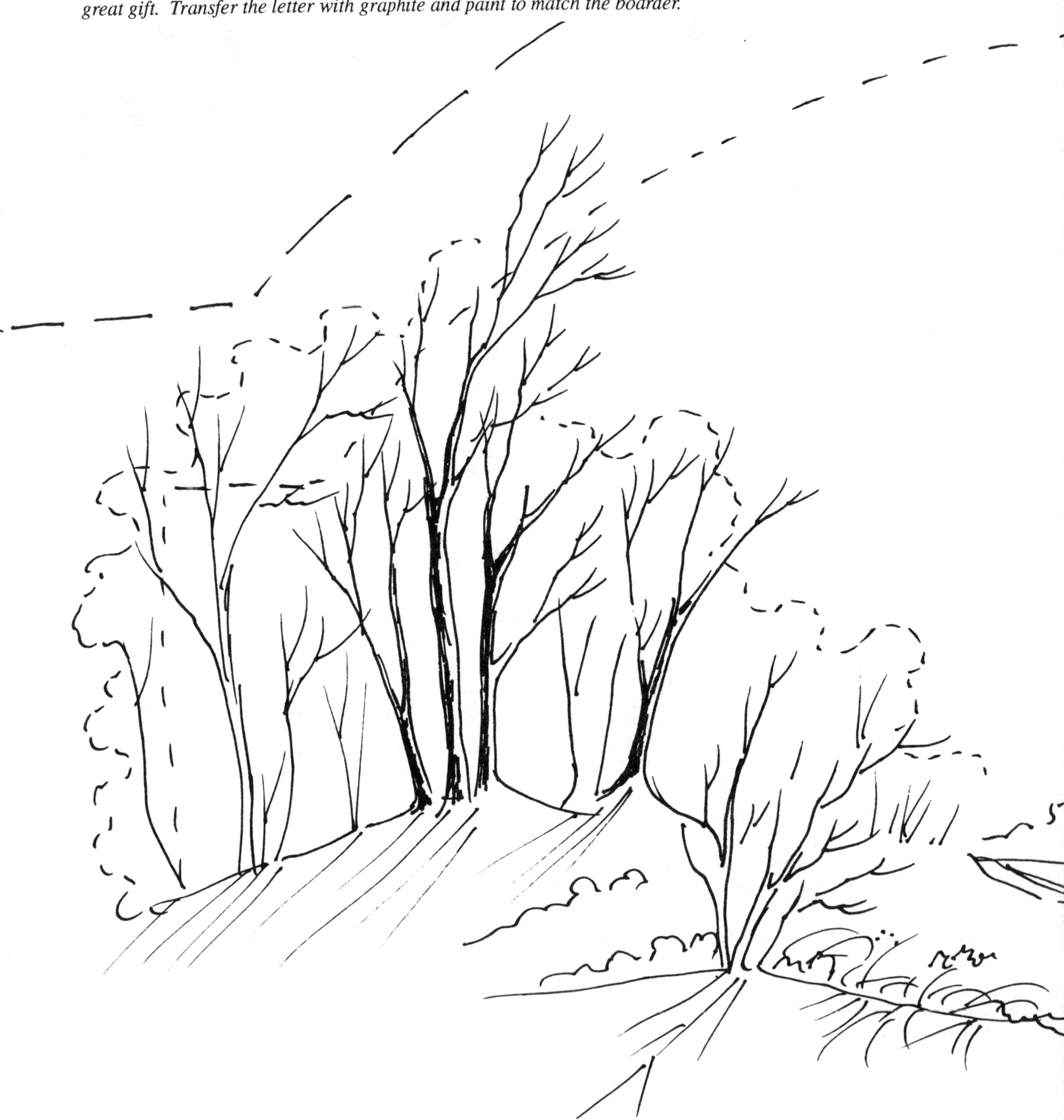

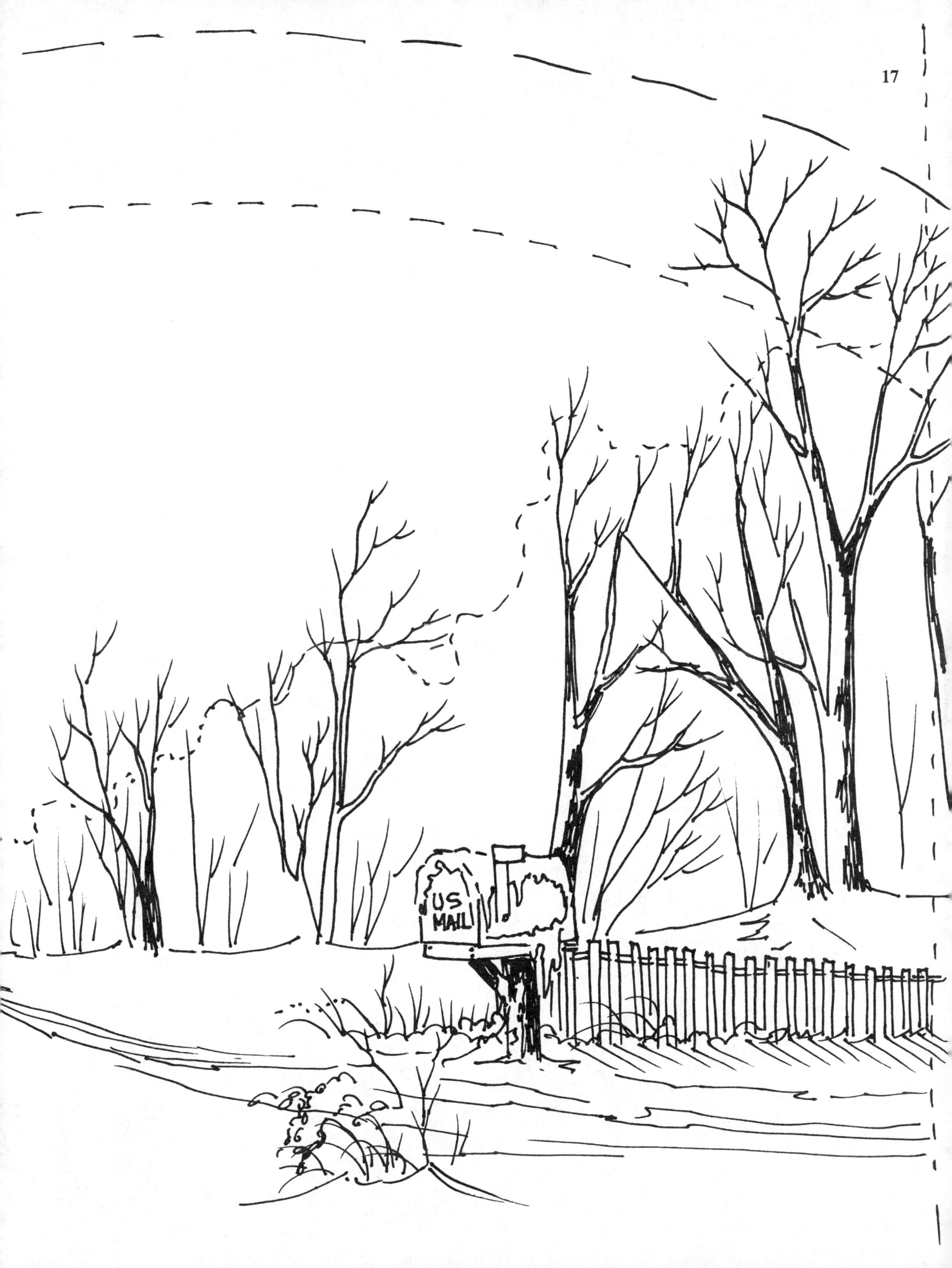
US
MAIL

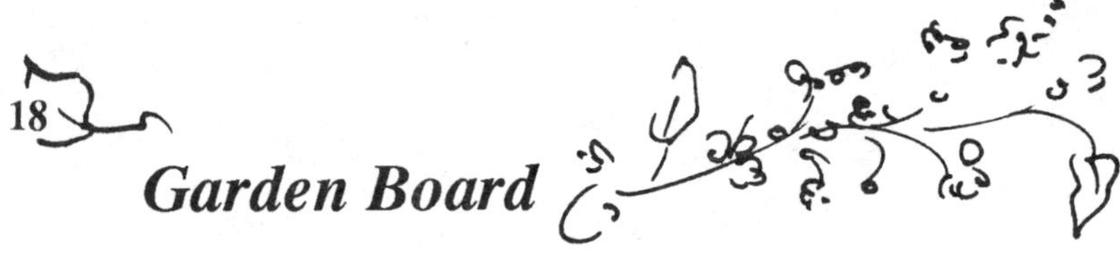

Garden Board

Surface; *Curved top wooden that you can easily cut your self. Adjust to fit any surface. Try on a Clip Board.*

Paints: *DecoArt Americana Acrylics*

Pick Colors of your choice and paint like your own garden refer to ***Flowers*** *section*

Attach a Post It pad. Pick a size and color pad to coordinate with your garden.

Hang from a satin ribbon to match.

Great Bazaar Item

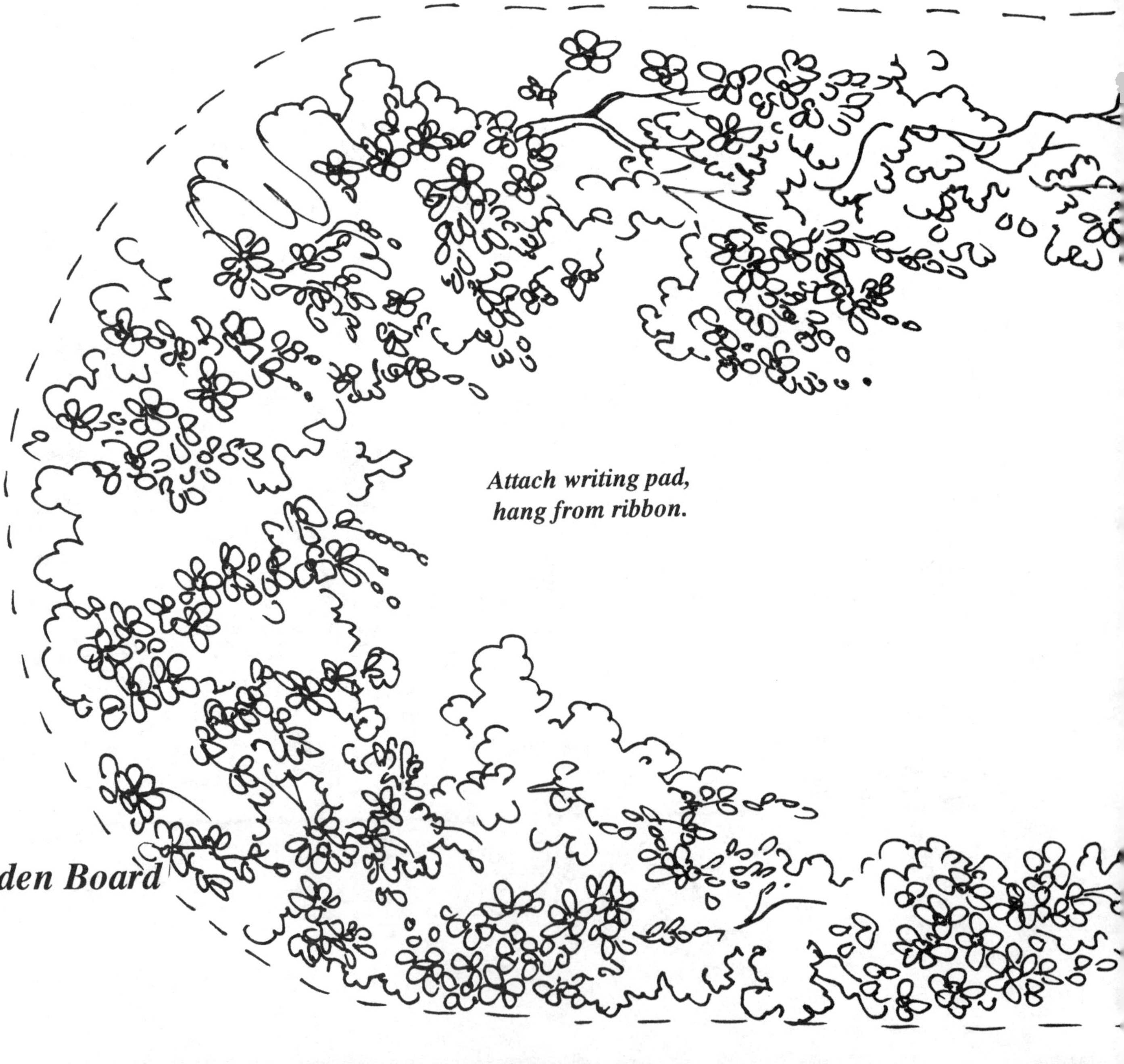

Attach writing pad,
hang from ribbon.

Garden Board

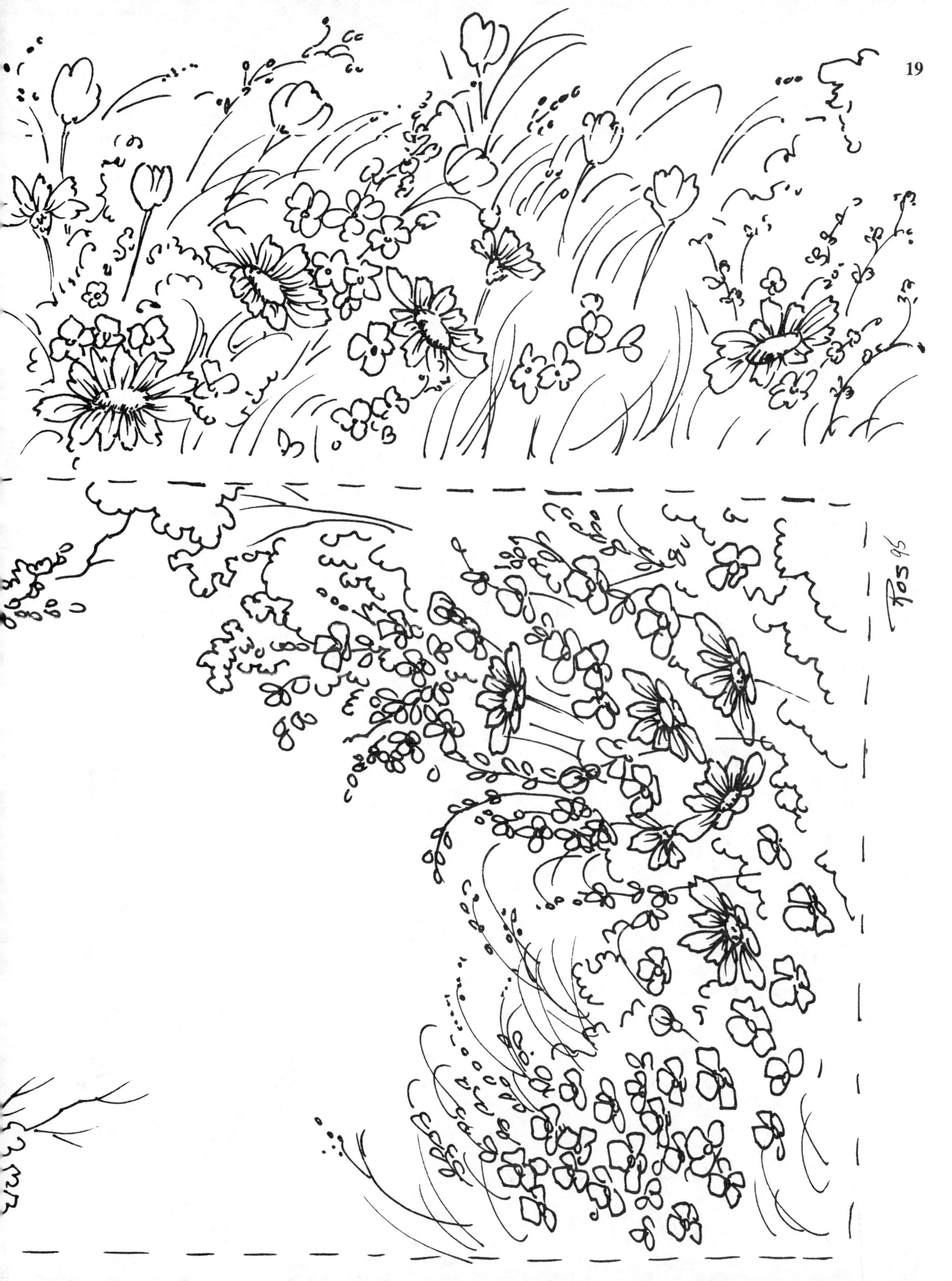

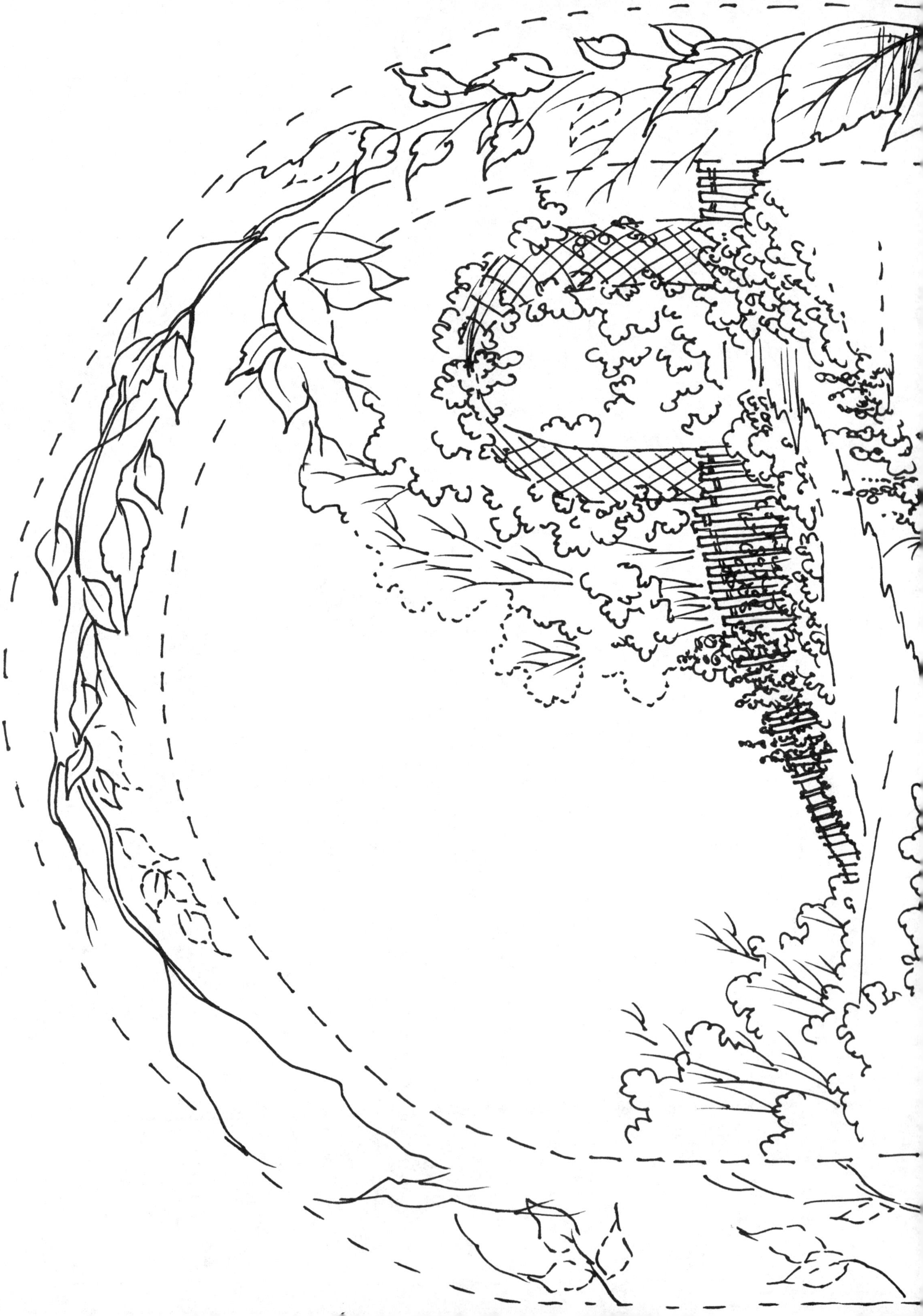

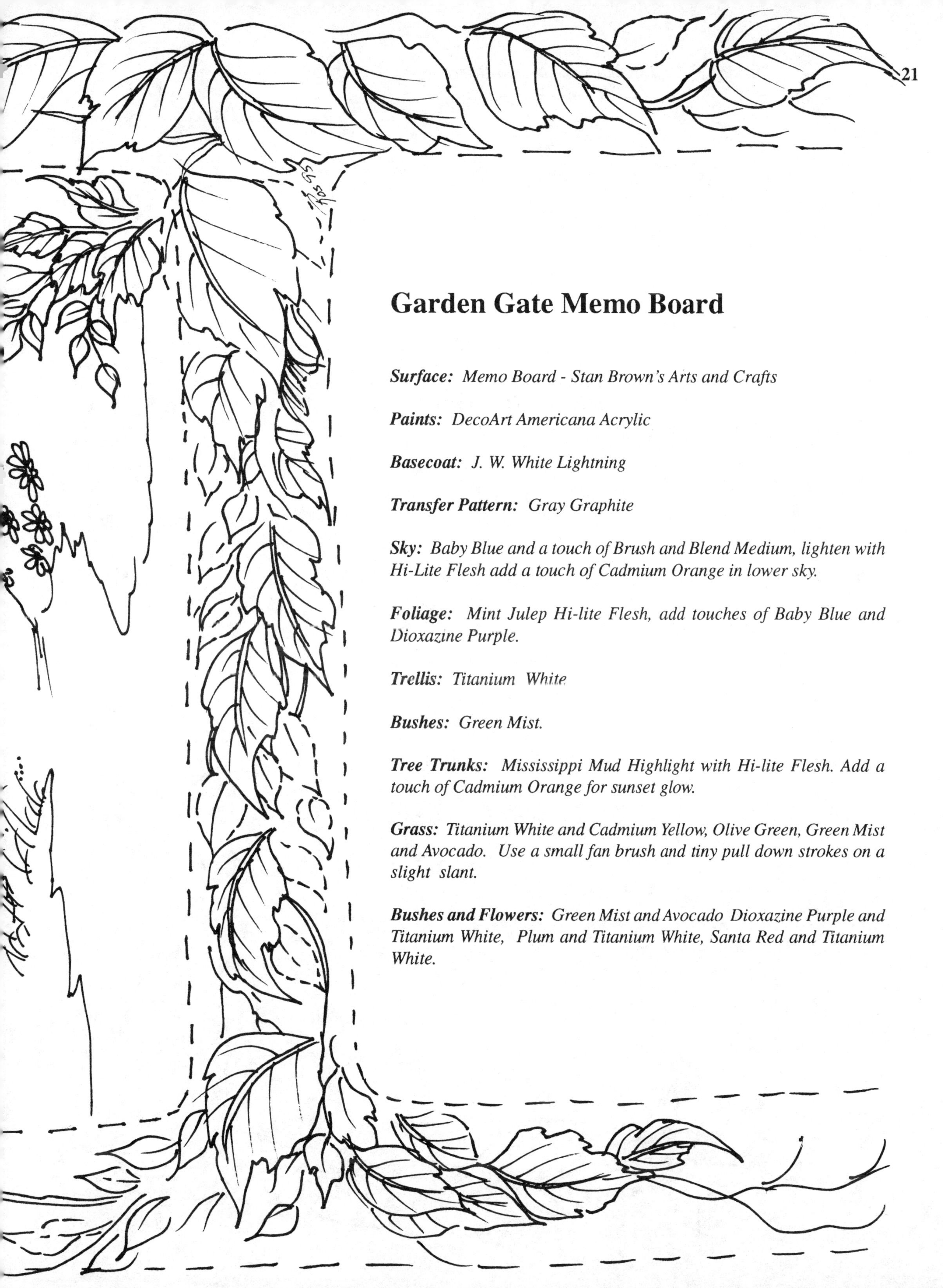

Garden Gate Memo Board

Surface: *Memo Board - Stan Brown's Arts and Crafts*

Paints: *DecoArt Americana Acrylic*

Basecoat: *J. W. White Lightning*

Transfer Pattern: *Gray Graphite*

Sky: *Baby Blue and a touch of Brush and Blend Medium, lighten with Hi-Lite Flesh add a touch of Cadmium Orange in lower sky.*

Foliage: *Mint Julep Hi-lite Flesh, add touches of Baby Blue and Dioxazine Purple.*

Trellis: *Titanium White*

Bushes: *Green Mist.*

Tree Trunks: *Mississippi Mud Highlight with Hi-lite Flesh. Add a touch of Cadmium Orange for sunset glow.*

Grass: *Titanium White and Cadmium Yellow, Olive Green, Green Mist and Avocado. Use a small fan brush and tiny pull down strokes on a slight slant.*

Bushes and Flowers: *Green Mist and Avocado Dioxazine Purple and Titanium White, Plum and Titanium White, Santa Red and Titanium White.*

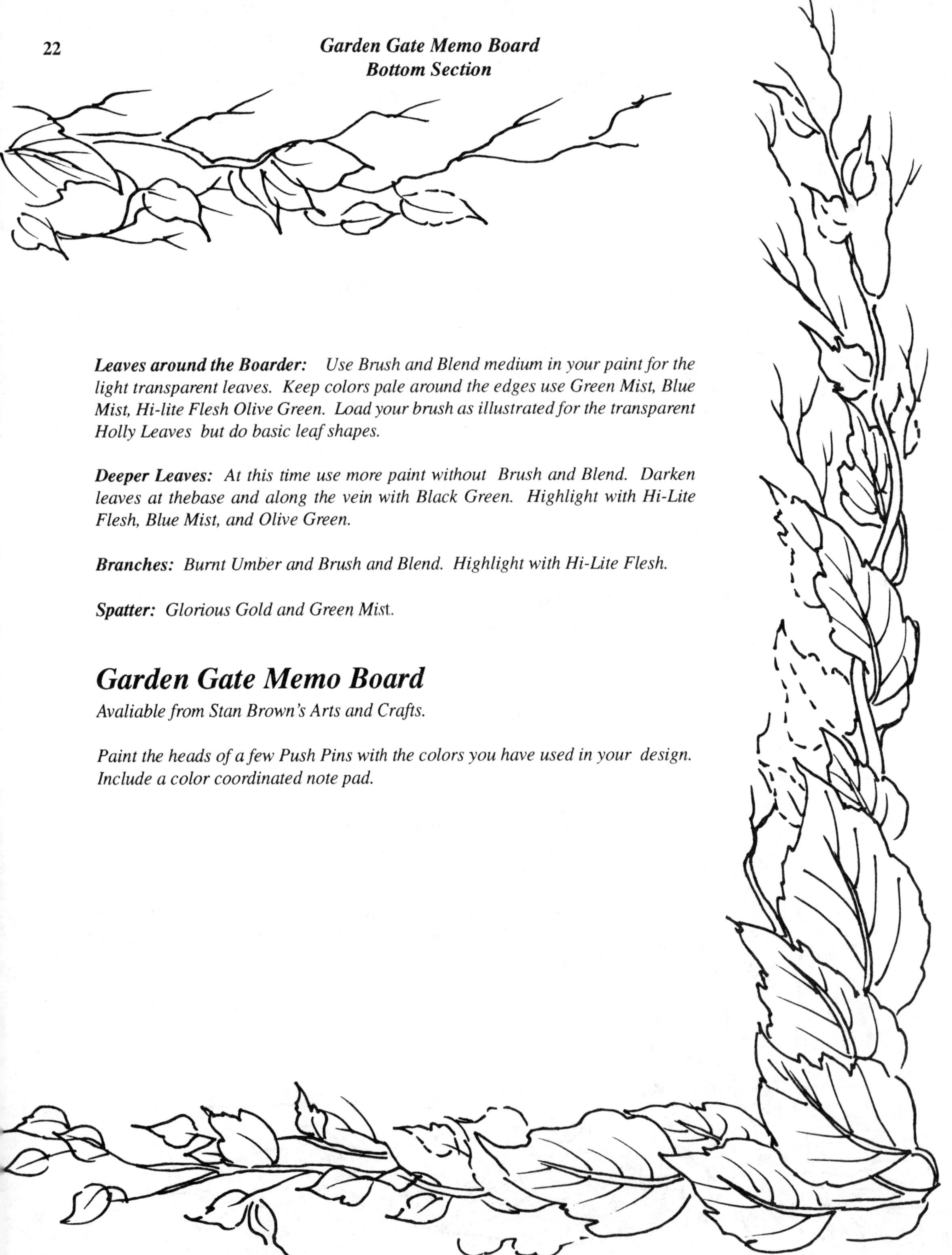

Leaves around the Boarder: *Use Brush and Blend medium in your paint for the light transparent leaves. Keep colors pale around the edges use Green Mist, Blue Mist, Hi-lite Flesh Olive Green. Load your brush as illustrated for the transparent Holly Leaves but do basic leaf shapes.*

Deeper Leaves: *At this time use more paint without Brush and Blend. Darken leaves at thebase and along the vein with Black Green. Highlight with Hi-Lite Flesh, Blue Mist, and Olive Green.*

Branches: *Burnt Umber and Brush and Blend. Highlight with Hi-Lite Flesh.*

Spatter: *Glorious Gold and Green Mist.*

Garden Gate Memo Board

Avaliable from Stan Brown's Arts and Crafts.

Paint the heads of a few Push Pins with the colors you have used in your design. Include a color coordinated note pad.

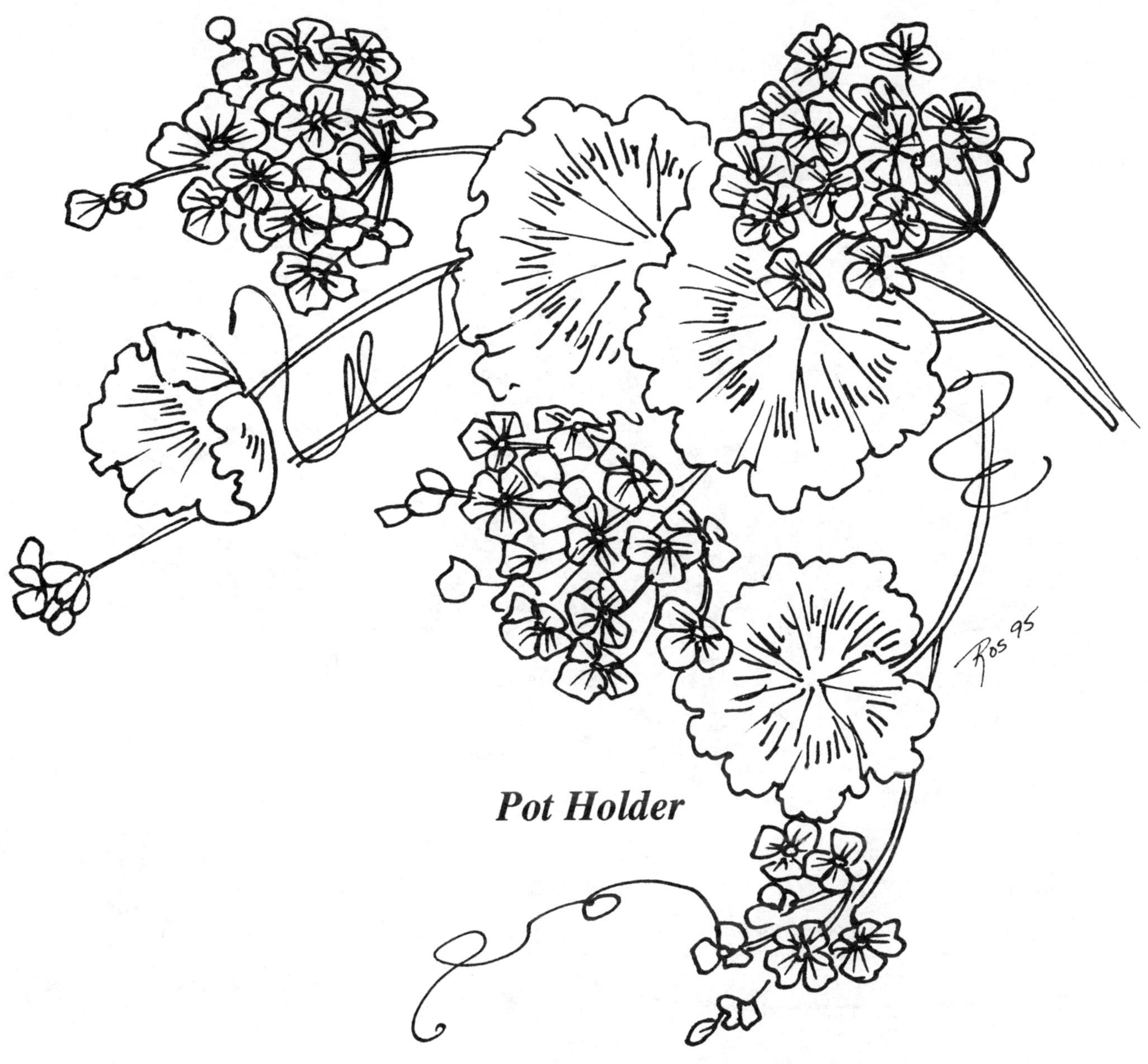

Pot Holder

Geraniums:

Surfaces: *Enamel Tray, Cups, Oven Mitt , Swith Plateand Pot Holder, Plaque*

Paint: *DecoArt Americana Acrylic, Ultra Gloss and So Soft Fabric Acrylic*

Leaves: *Base with Avocado, Shade with Evergreen and Paynes Gray. Highlight with Olive Green.*

Flowers: *Base with Napa Red Highlight petals with Cherry Red and Cadmium Orange.*

Stems and Squiggles: *Avocado or other shade of green to show up against your background color.*

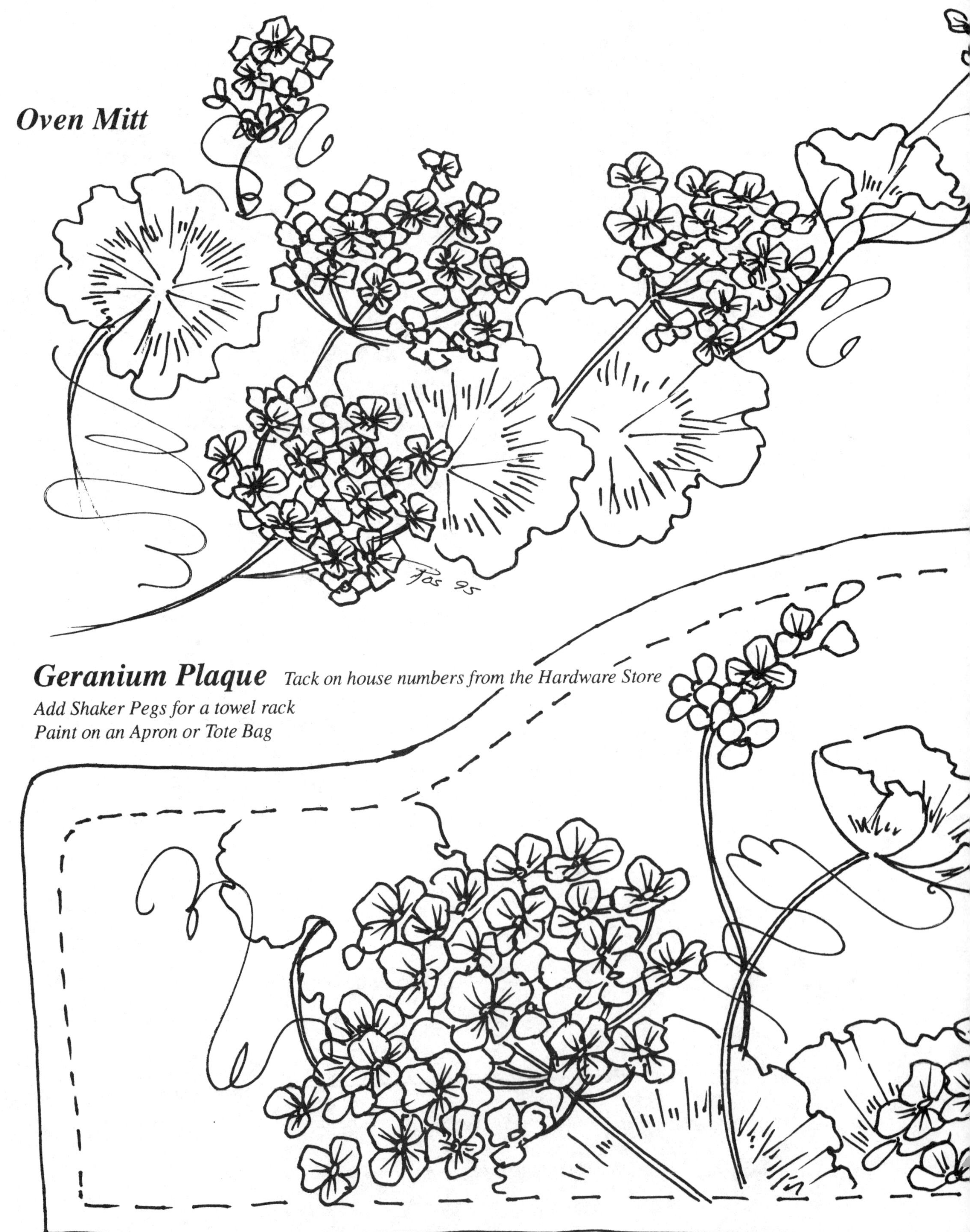
Oven Mitt
Jos 95
Geranium Plaque *Tack on house numbers from the Hardware Store*
Add Shaker Pegs for a towel rack
Paint on an Apron or Tote Bag

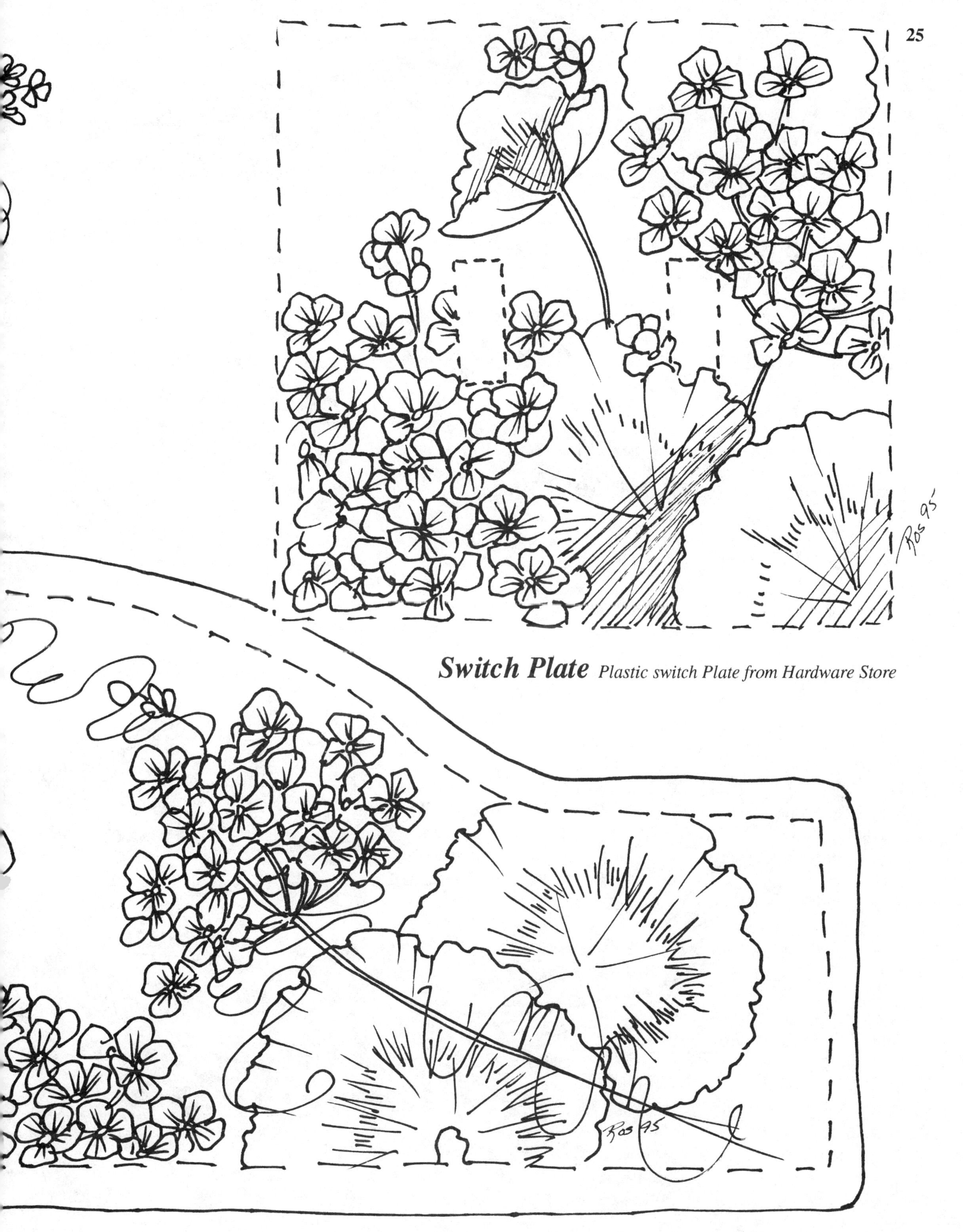

Switch Plate *Plastic switch Plate from Hardware Store*

Pyrcantha Plate

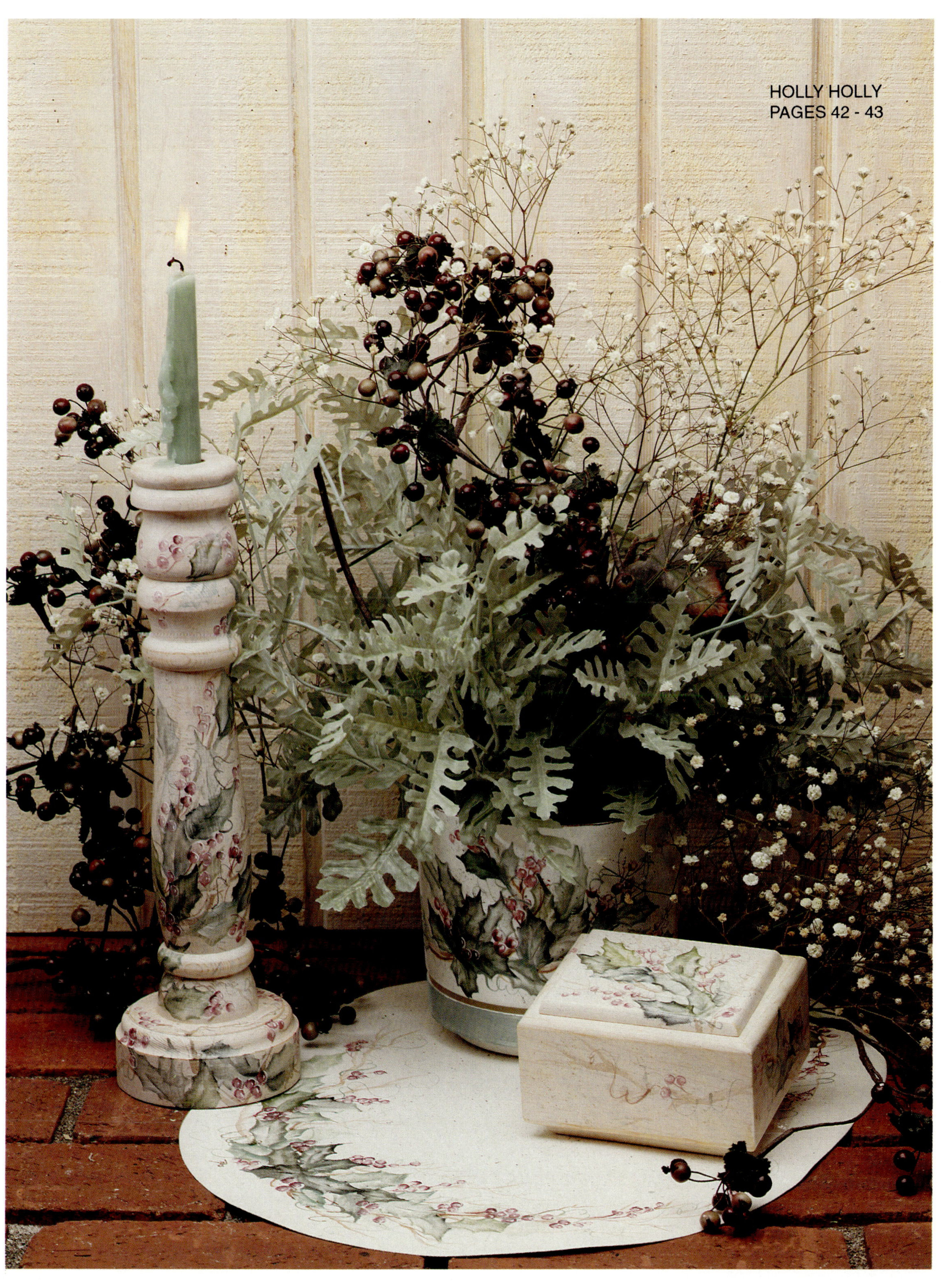
HOLLY HOLLY
PAGES 42 - 43

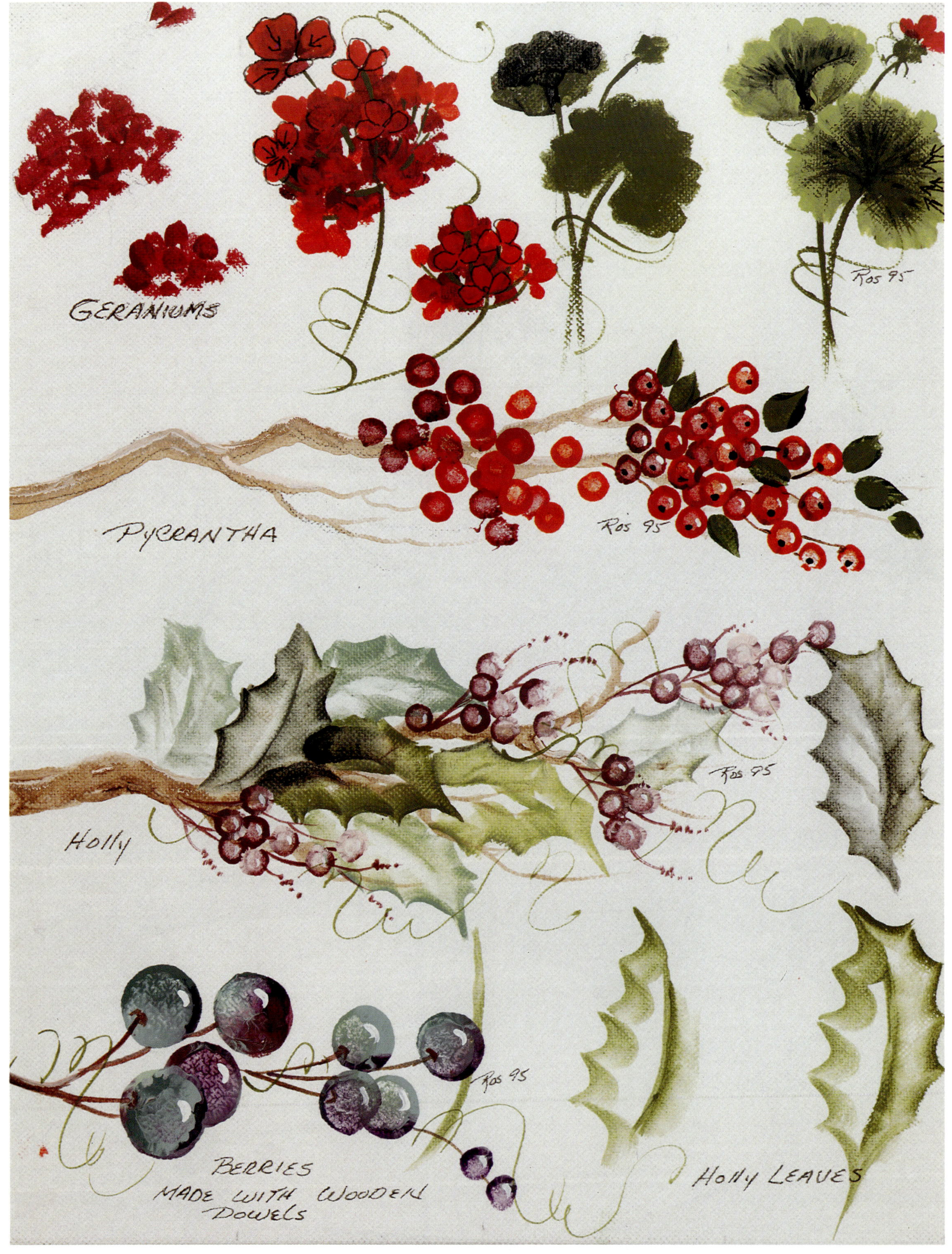
GERANIUMS
Ros 95
PYCRANTHA
Ros 95
Ros 95
Holly
Ros 95
BERRIES
MADE WITH WOODEN
DOWELS
Holly LEAVES

Pyracantha

Surfaces: *Ceramic Lamp and Shade, Apron, Wooden Plate, Placemat, and Napkins*

Paint: *DecoArt Americana, Ultra Gloss, and So Soft Fabric Paint*

Branches: *Burnt Umber Highlight with Hi Lite Flesh.*

Leaves: *Avocado, Evergreen, Evergreen and Paynes Gray, and Olive Green Squishy Leaves or Stroke Leaves with the edge of a filbert brush.*

Berries: *Napa Red, Cherry Red, and Cadmium Orange. Highlight with Whit.e. Black dots are on some.*

Ribbons: *Base with Cherry Red undercoat on dark background with White as necessary. Shade with Napa Red. Highlight with White.*

Pine Needles: *Avocado, Evergreen, Olive Green. Chisel edge of angle shader or liner brush.*

Squiggles: *Avocado*

Note: *Colors noted are for Americana Acrylics. Adjust colors when using Ultra Gross or So Soft Fabric Paints. Use Avocado and Black for a dark value and Avocado and Yellow for a light value. Christmas Red and Dioxazine Purple make a good dark Value for the berries.*

Try some of these berries on a Ornament

Guest Towel

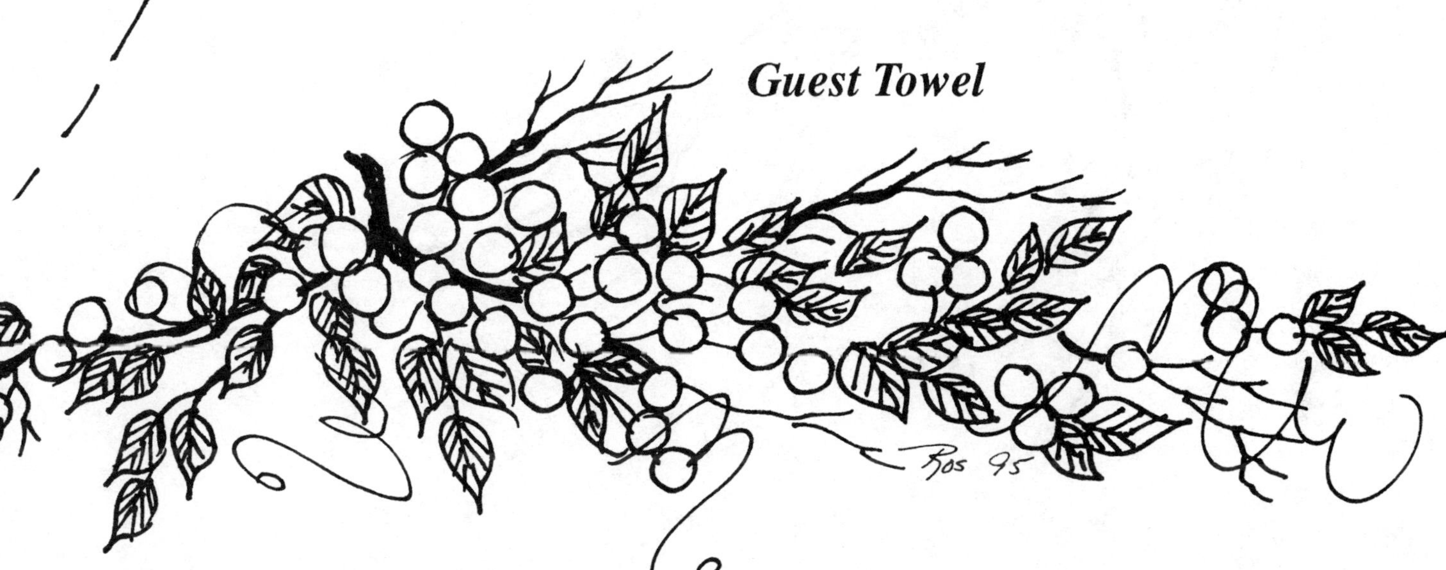

Pyracantha
Placemat or Wooden Platter
Fredrix Canvas   Walnut Hollow

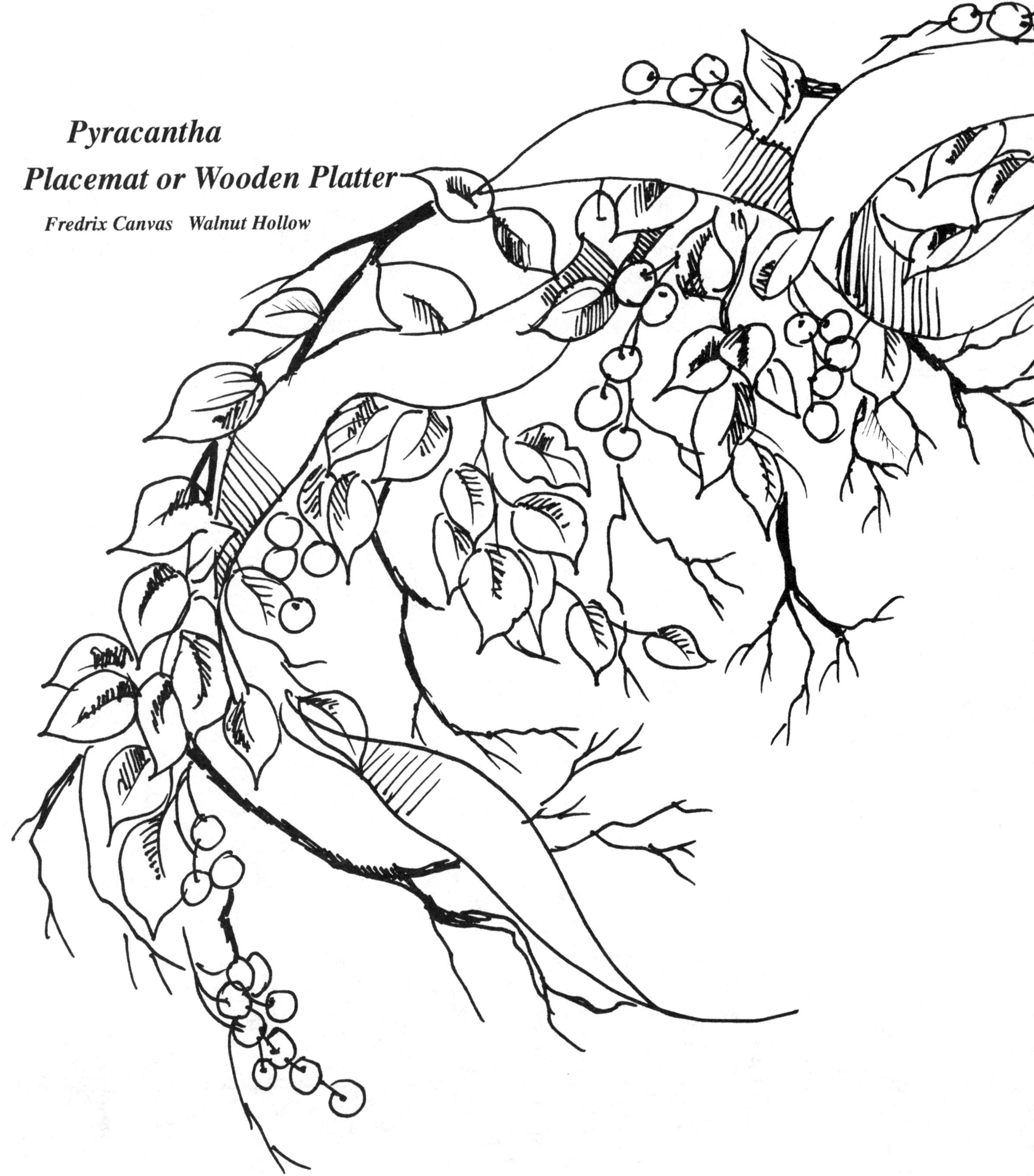

Oval Wooden Platter
available from
Walnut Hollow

Also use placemat and
add pine needles.

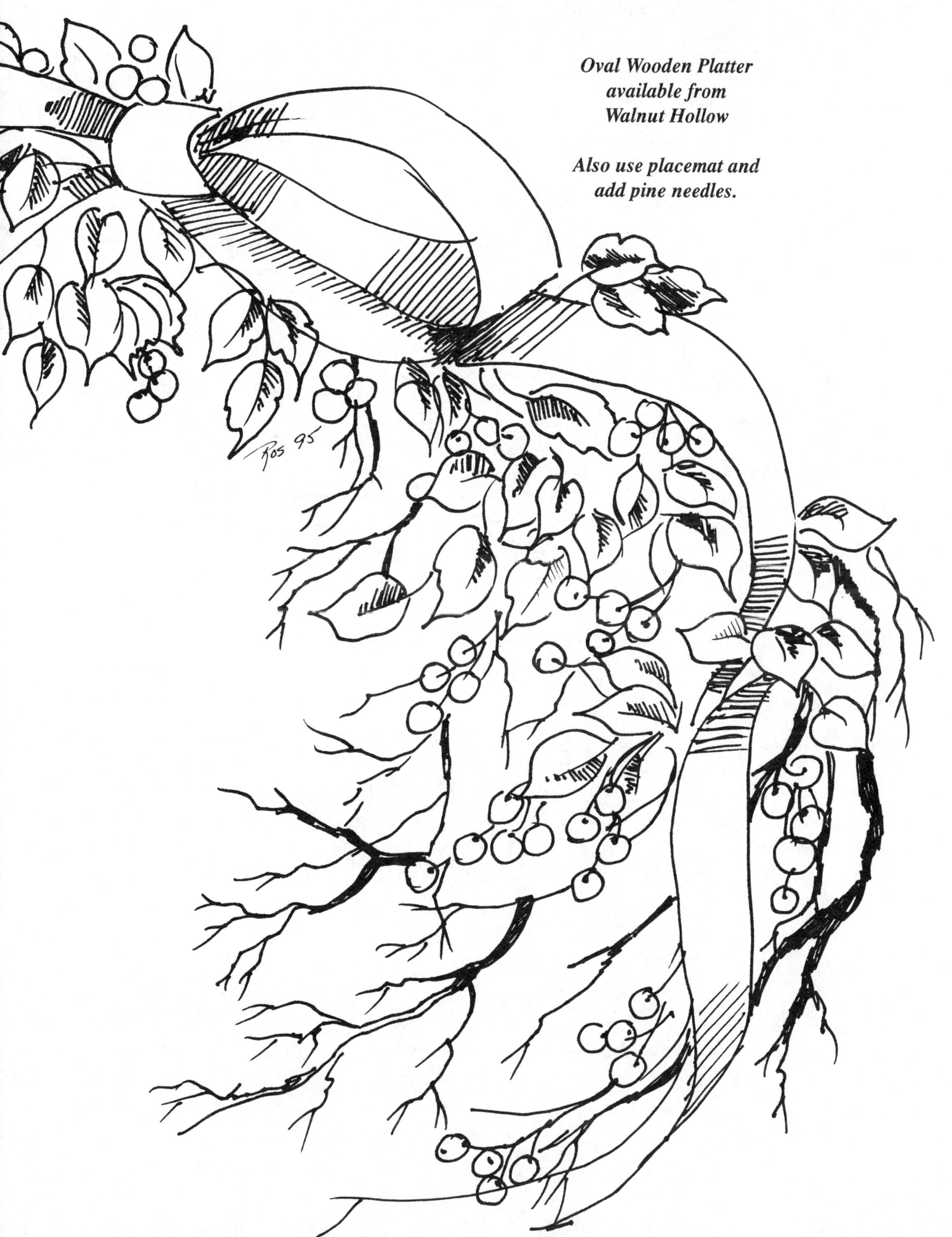

Repeat berries and squishy leaves up white candlestick.

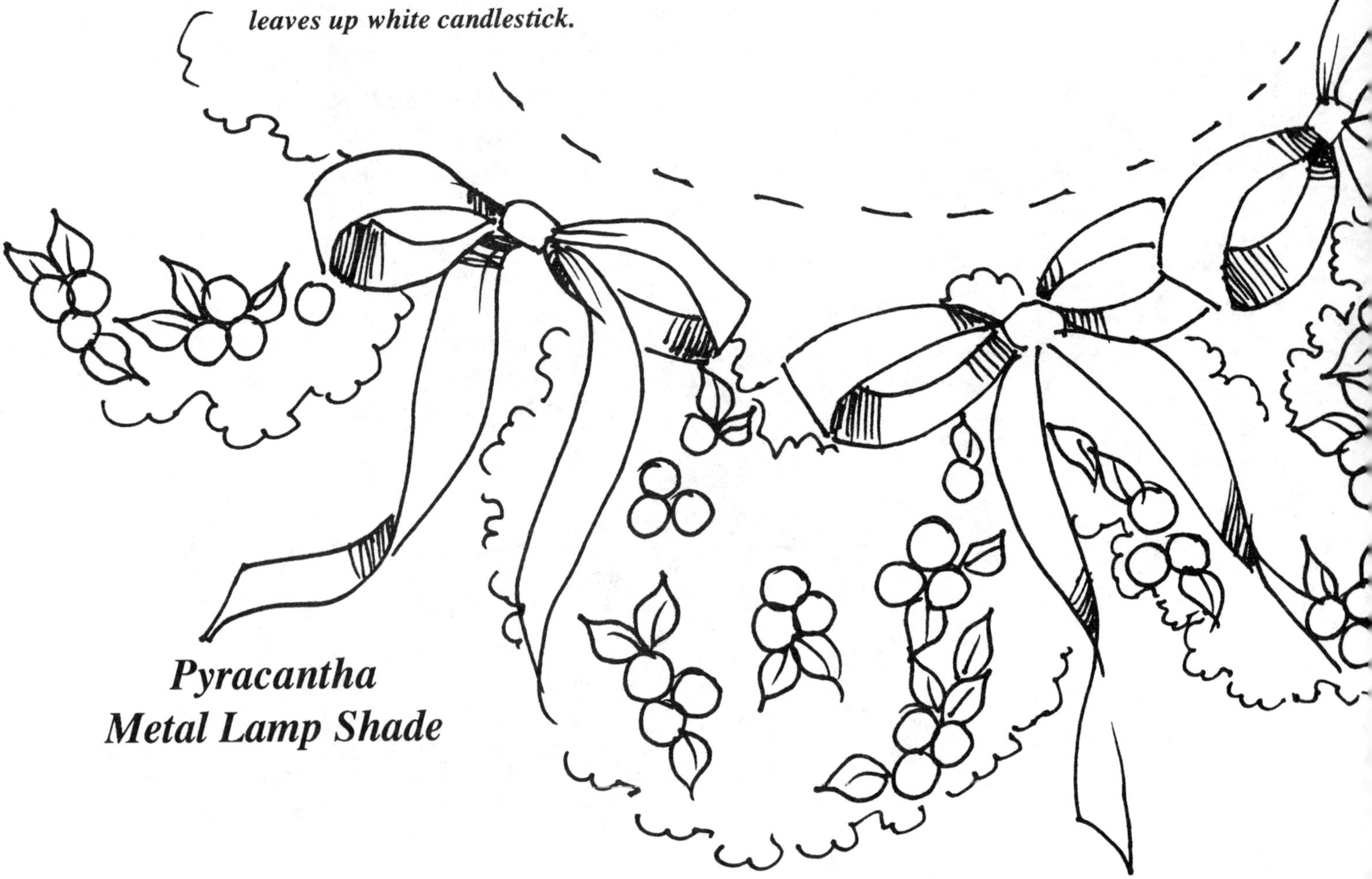

Pyracantha Metal Lamp Shade

Pyracantha Lamp Shade

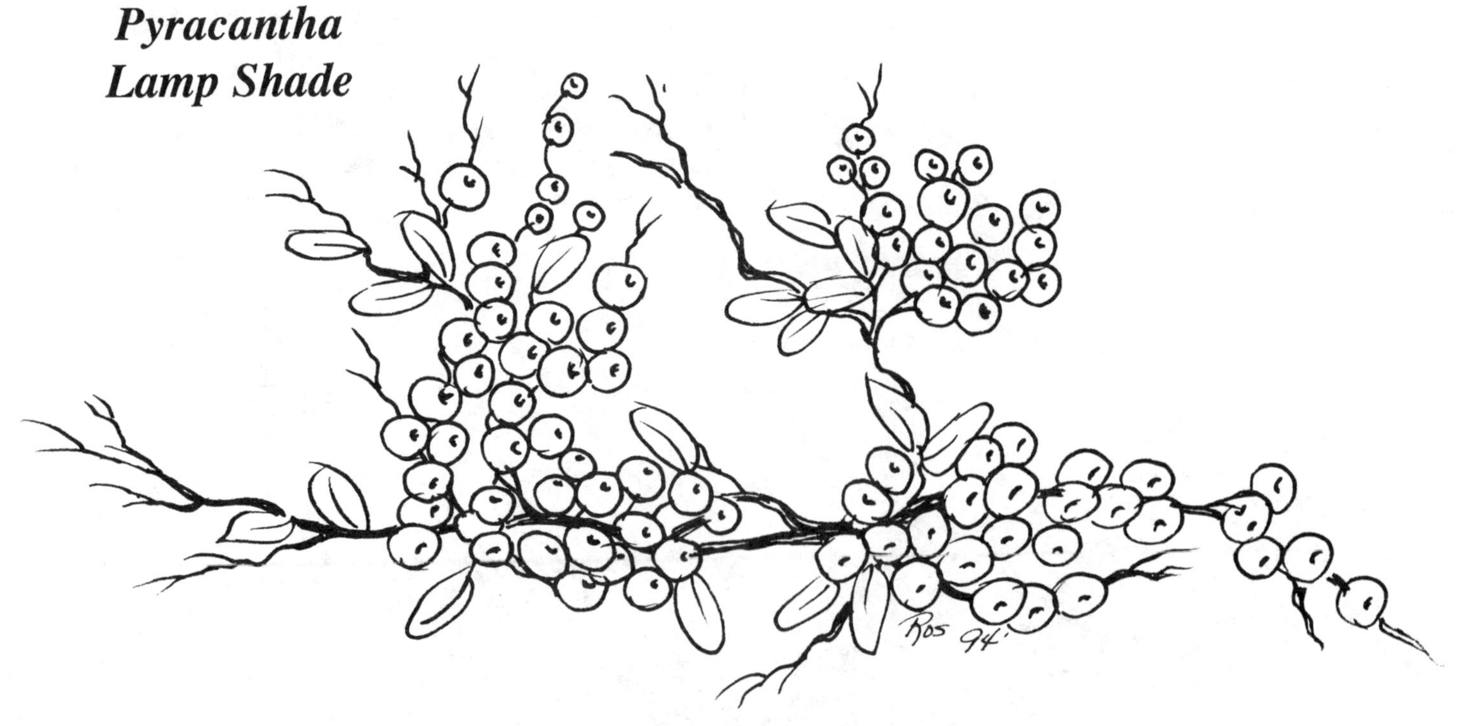

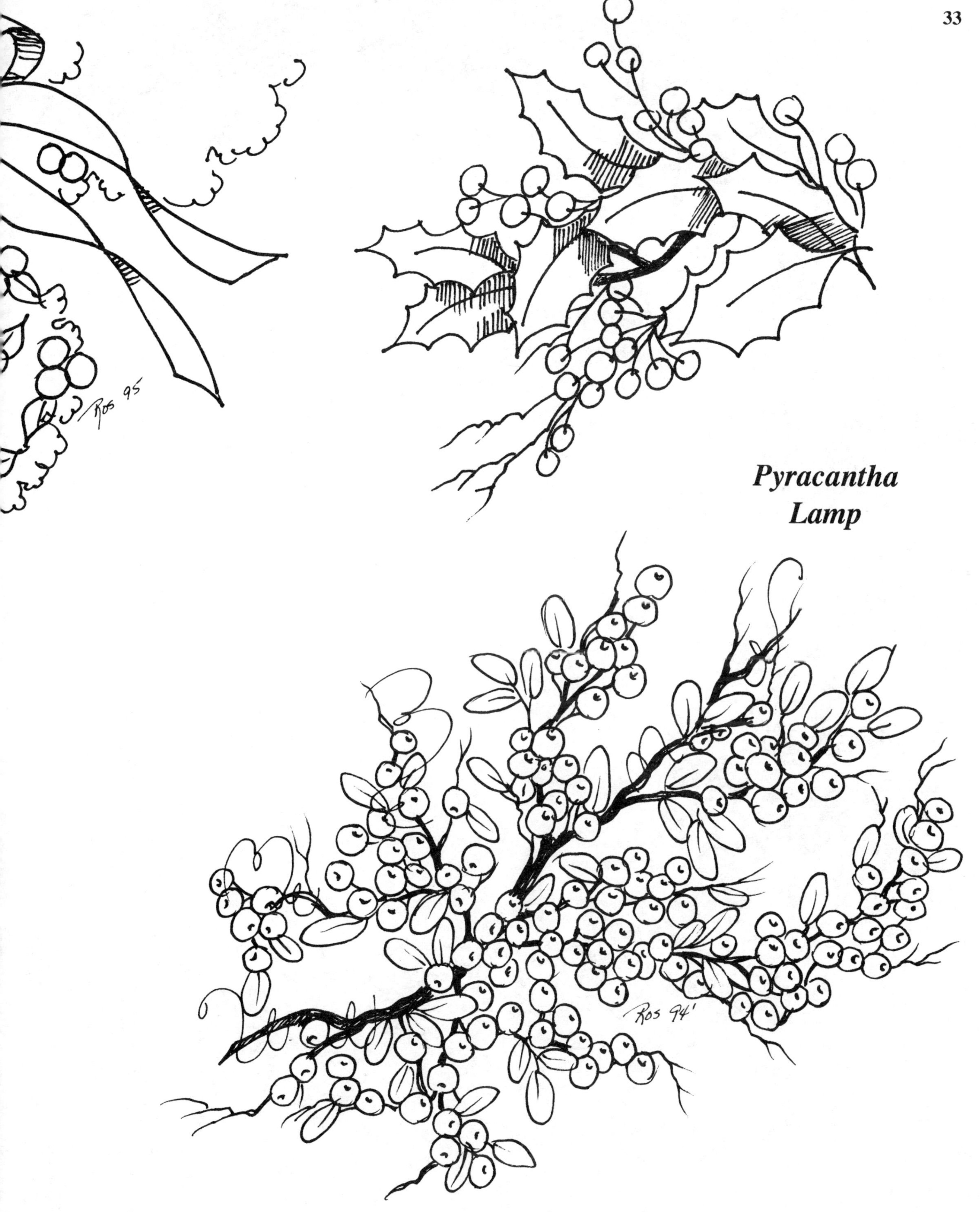

Pyracantha Lamp

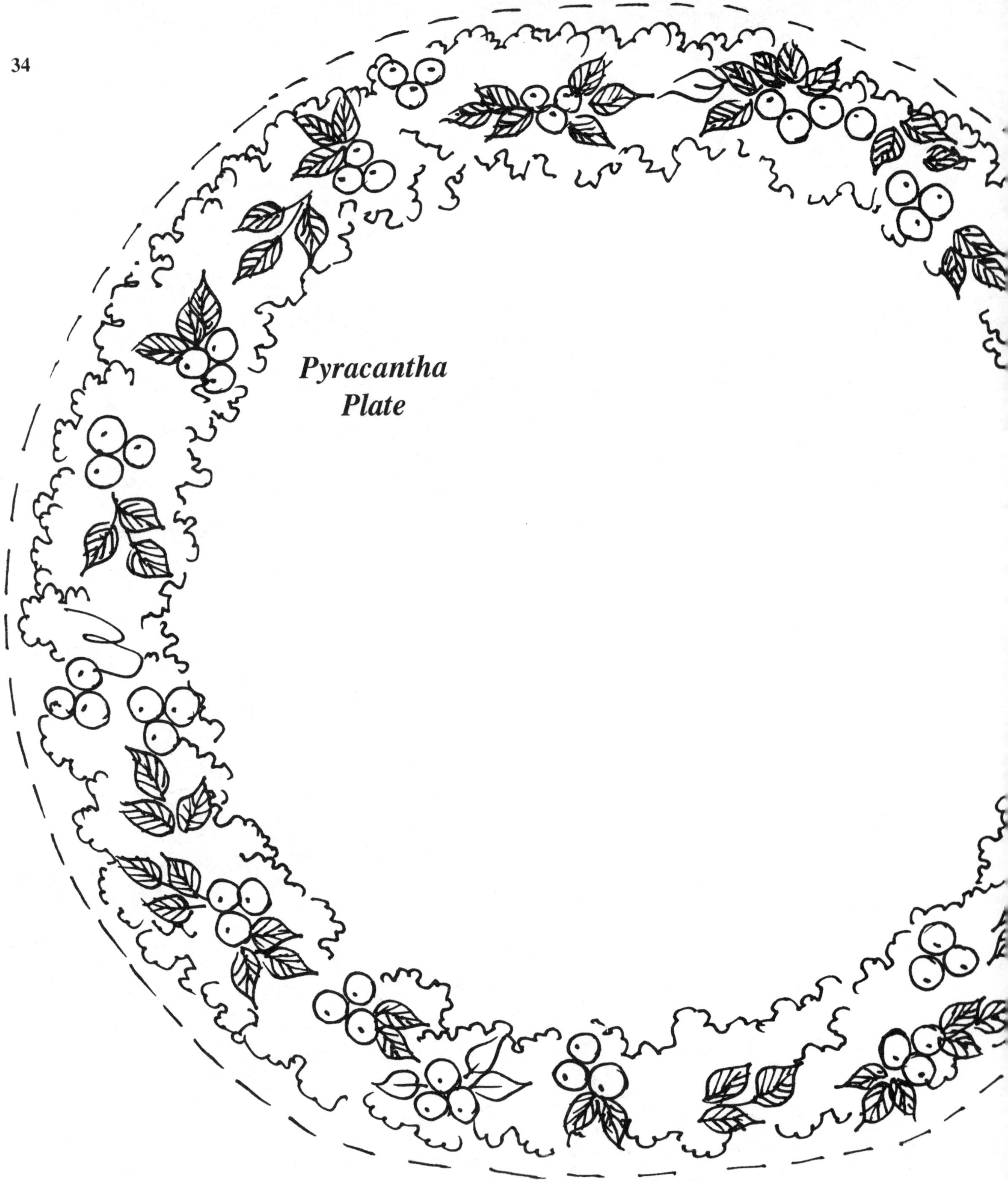

Pyracantha Plate

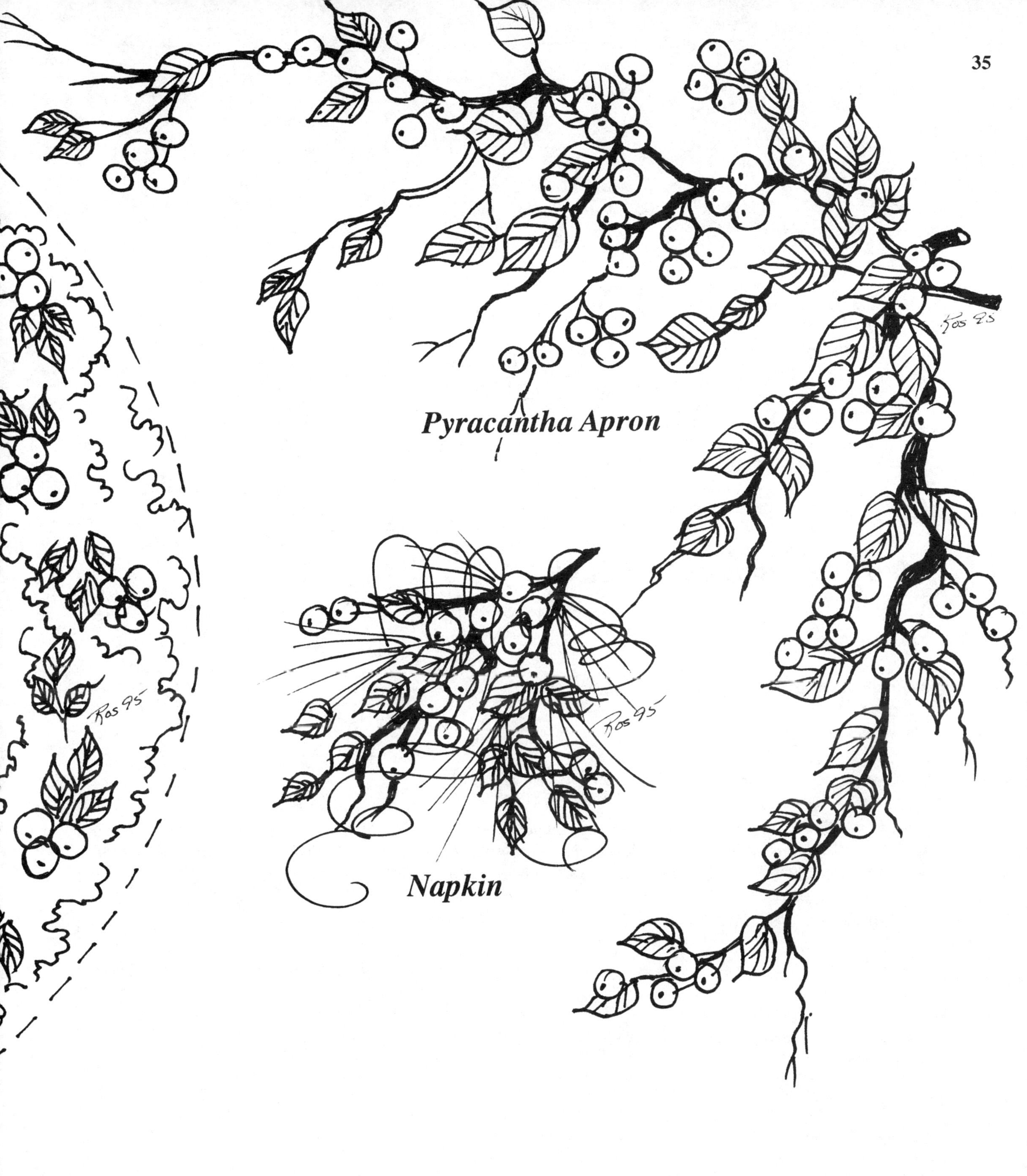
Ros 95
Pyracantha Apron
Ros 95
Ros 95
Napkin

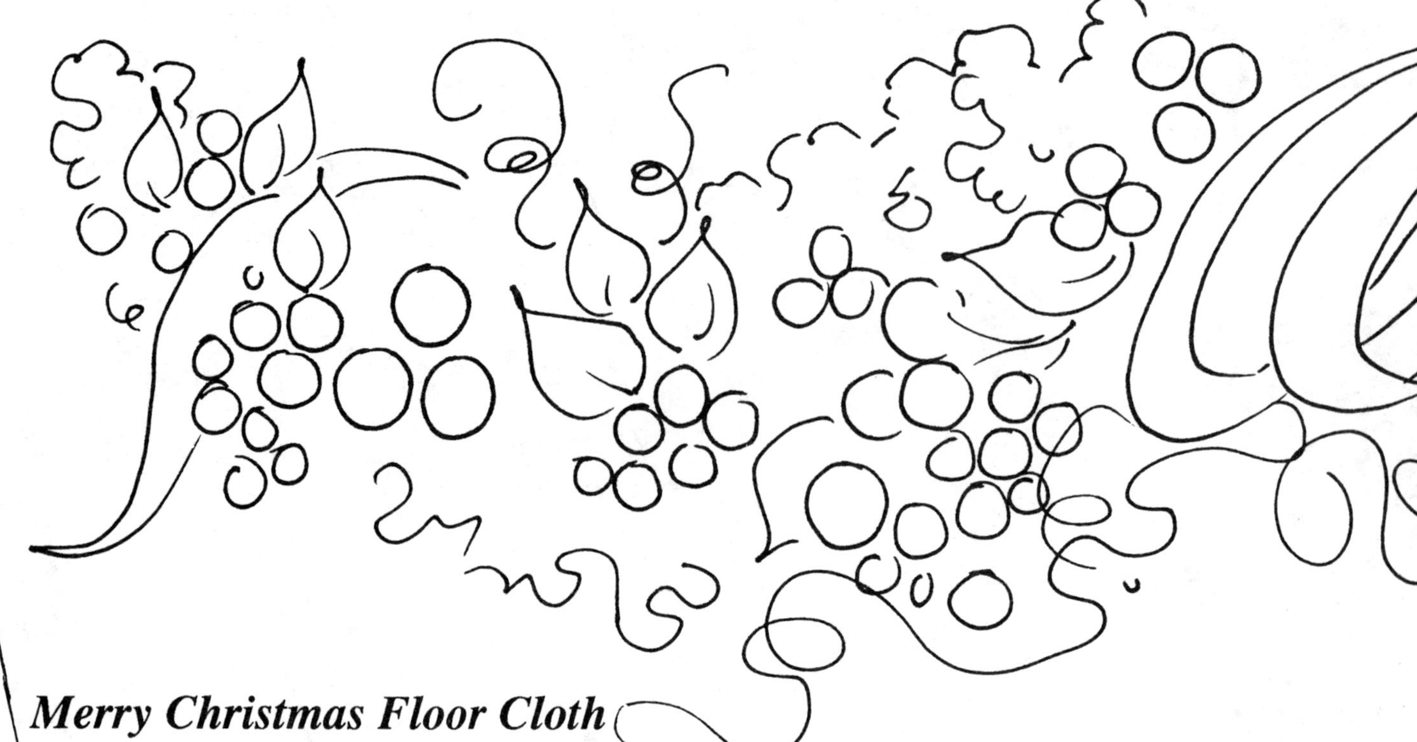

Merry Christmas Floor Cloth

Surface: *Canvas Floor Cloth - Fredrix*

Paint: *DecoArt Americana Acrylic*

Basecoat: *Black Forest Green two coats*

Foliage: *Avocado, Black Forest Green, Olive Green and Teal.*

Letters and Bows: *My Special thanks to Camile Scheewe who beautifully lettered this floor cloth for me to share with you all.. Transfer lettering and bows with white graphite. Undercoat with Titanium White allow to dry, Repaint with Cherry Red. Shade with Napa Red and a little Dioxazine Purple. Highlight with Titanium White.*

Squishy Leaves: *1/2 inch flat brush. Black Forest Green, Avocado, Olive Green.*

Holly Berries: *Napa Red, Dioxazine Purple, Cherry Red, and Cadmium Orange. Highlight with Titanium White.*

Bayberries: *1/2 inch wooden dowel Olive Green, Green Mist, and Teal.*

Stems: *Burnt Umber and Titanium White.*

Squiggles: *Olive Green*

Varnish: *Three coats of J. W. Right Step Varnish.*

Would look great on anyone's floor.

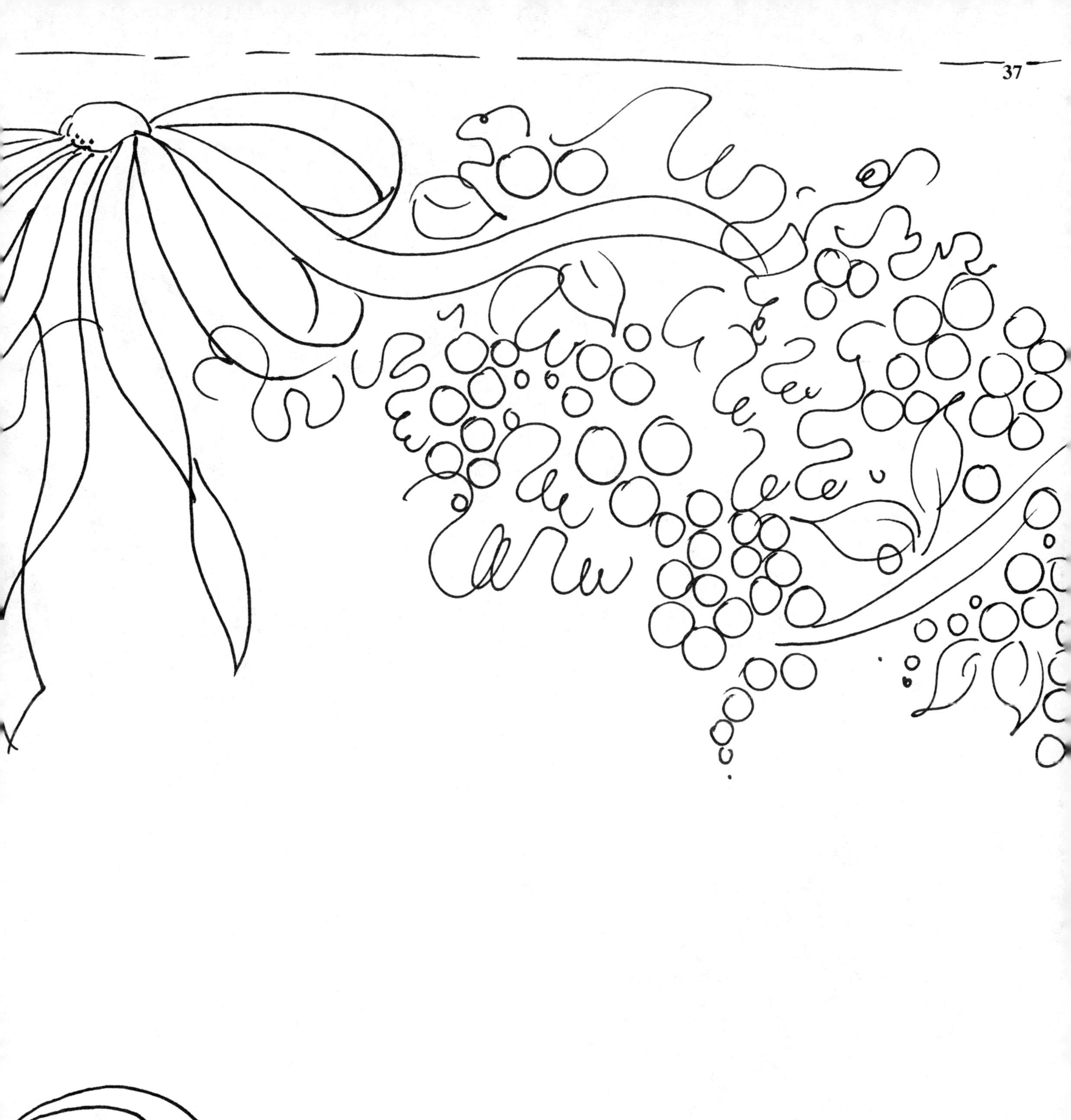

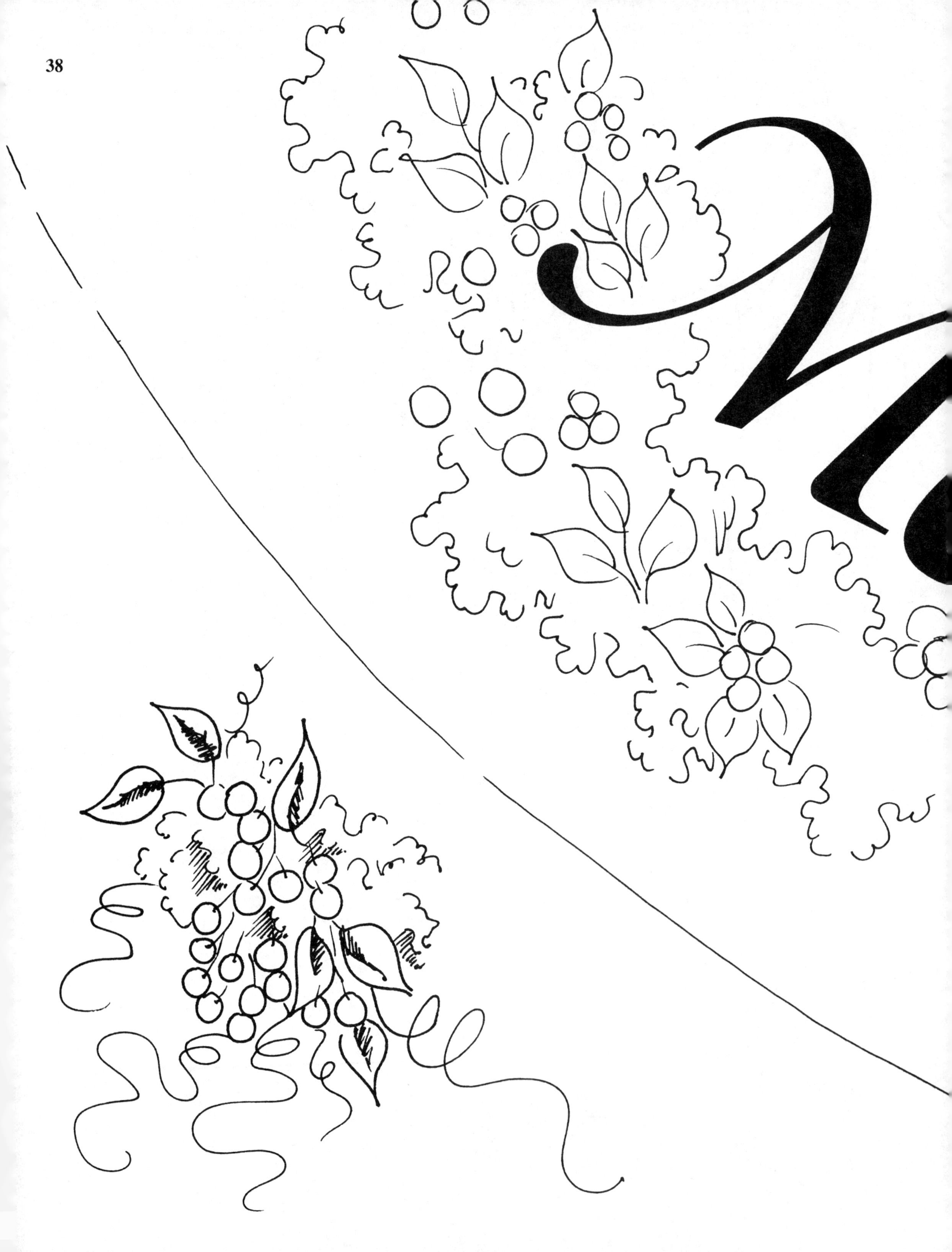

Merry Christmas Floor Cloth

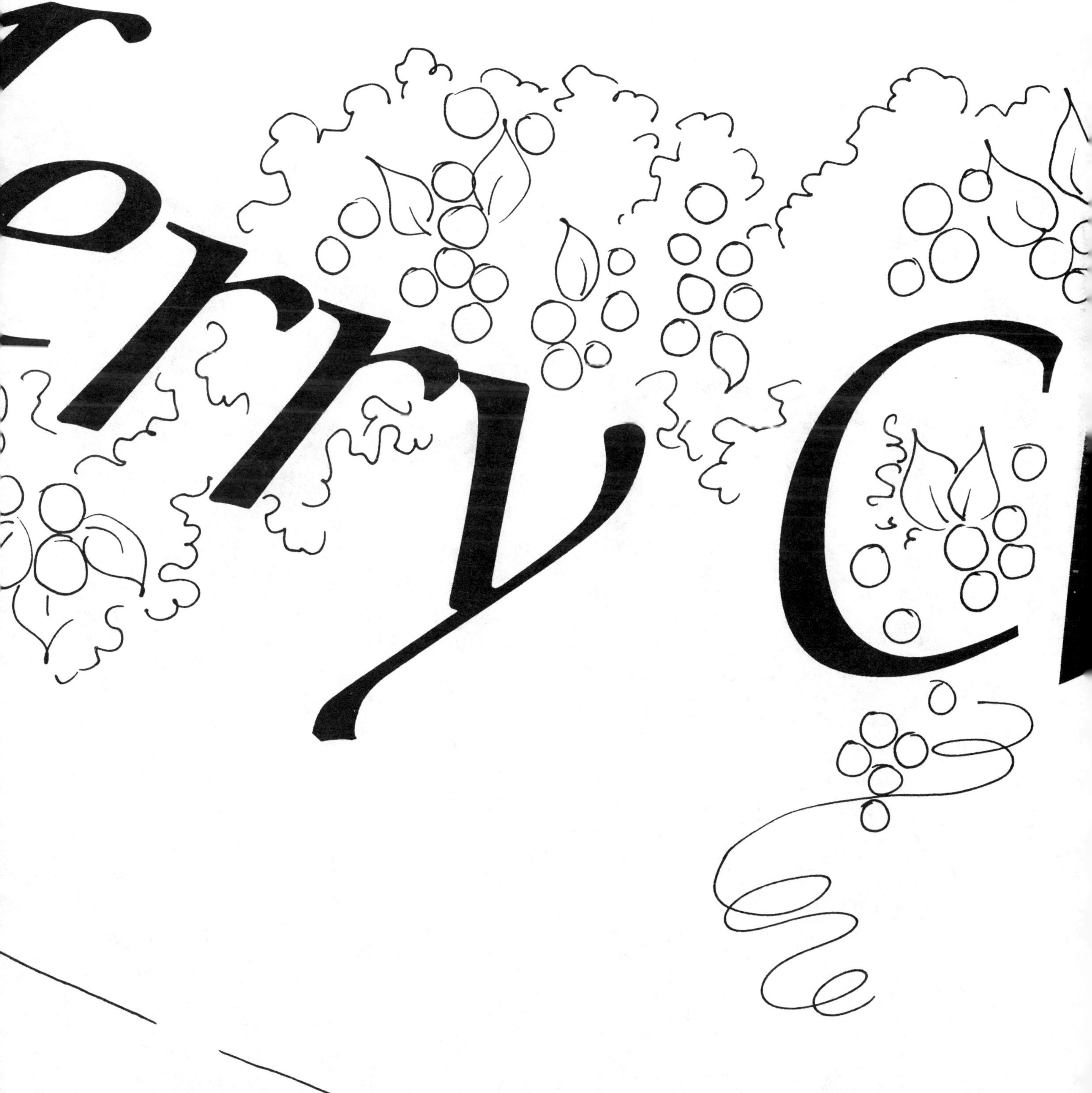

Merry Christmas Floor Cloth

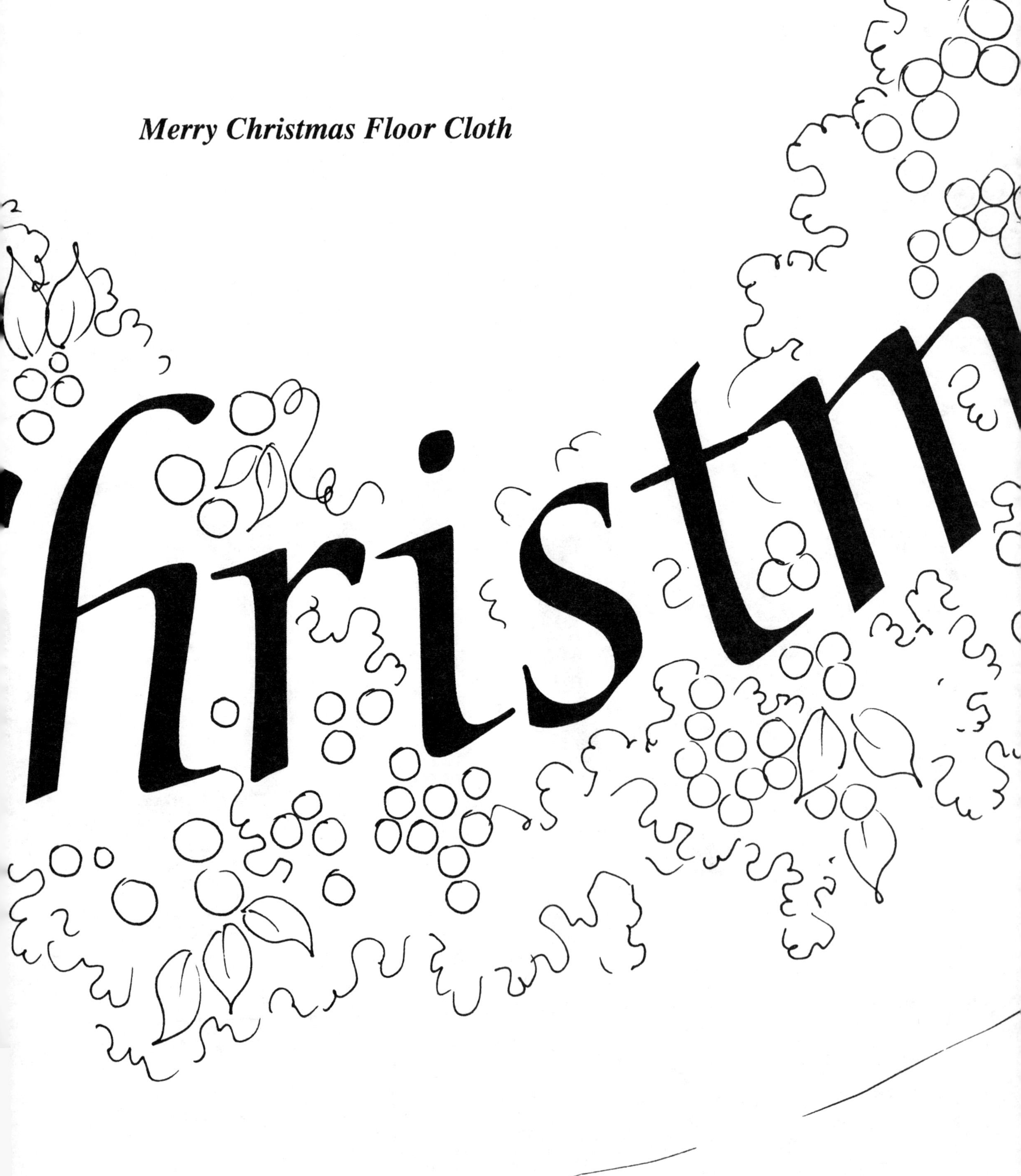

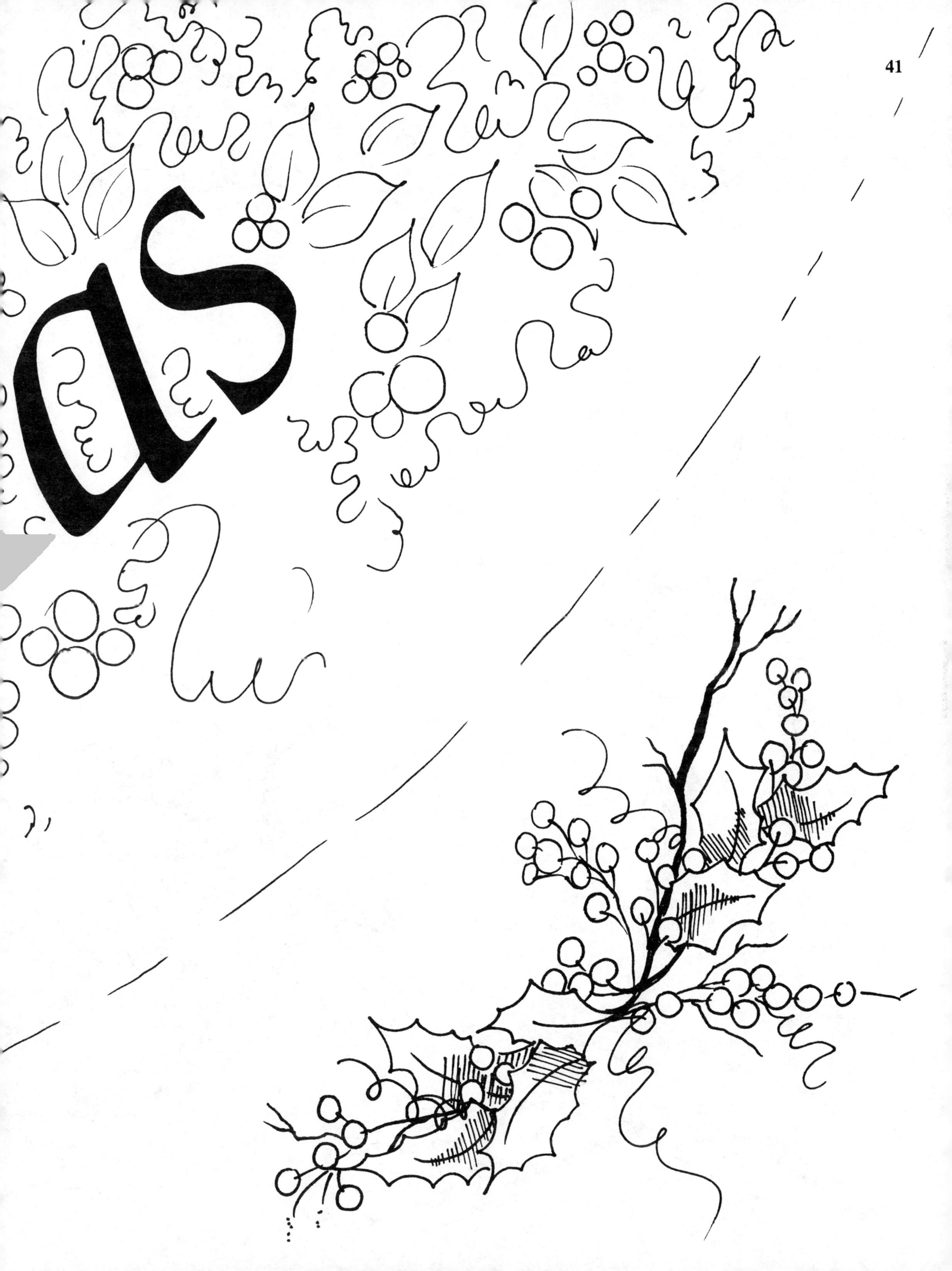

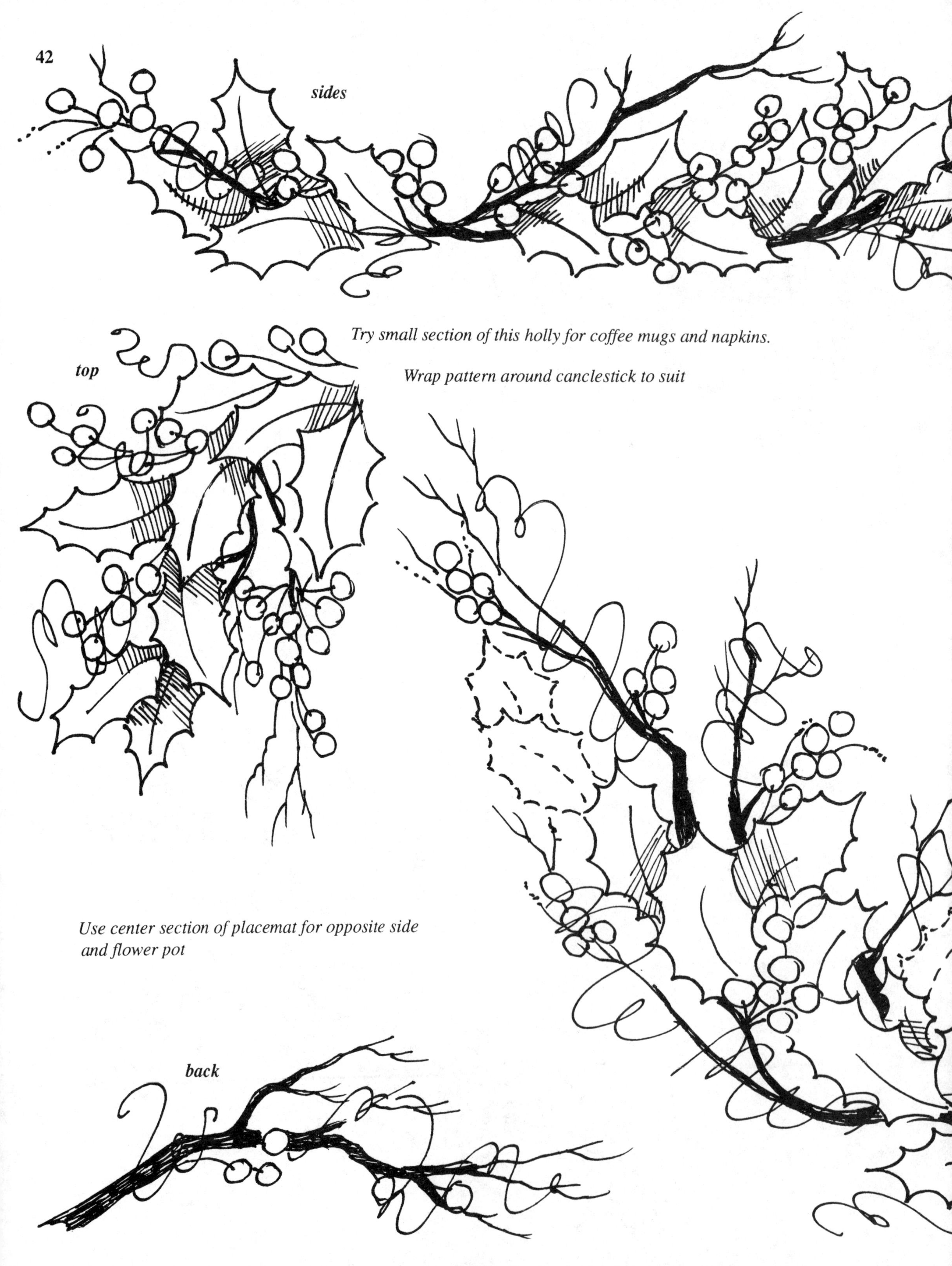

Try small section of this holly for coffee mugs and napkins.

Wrap pattern around canclestick to suit

Use center section of placemat for opposite side and flower pot

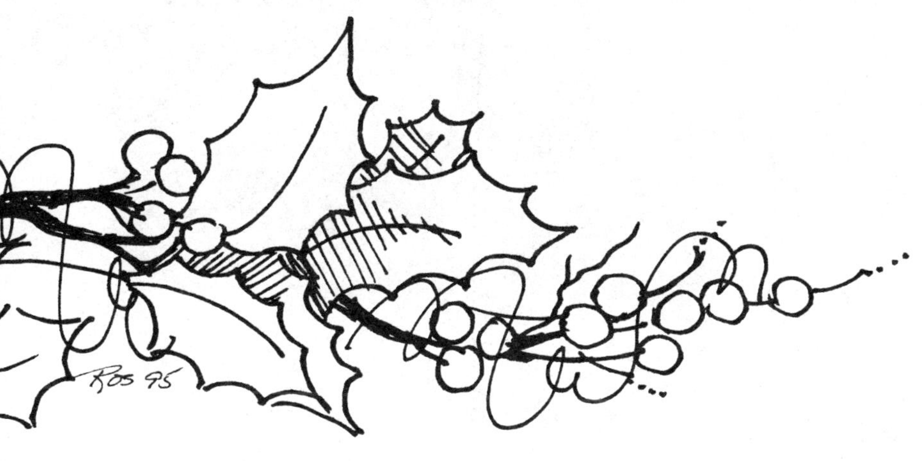

Holly Holly

Surfaces: *Wooden Candlestick, Wooden Box - Stan Brown's Arts and Crafts*
Canvas Placemat - Fredrix Canvas
Plastic Flower Pot - Hardware Store

Paint: *DecoArt Americana Acrylic*

Branches: *Burnt Umber, Highlight with Hi Lite Flesh*

Leaves: *Paint leaves with assorted colors using Black Green, Avocado, Green Mist, Blue Mist, Olive Green and Mint Julep.*

Berries: *Tap Berries with Plum and Plum and Hi Lite Flesh. Highlight berries with Titanium White.*

Stems and squiggles: *Green Mist or Mint Julep*

Spatter: *Use an old tooth brush - Glorious Gold and Green Mist.*

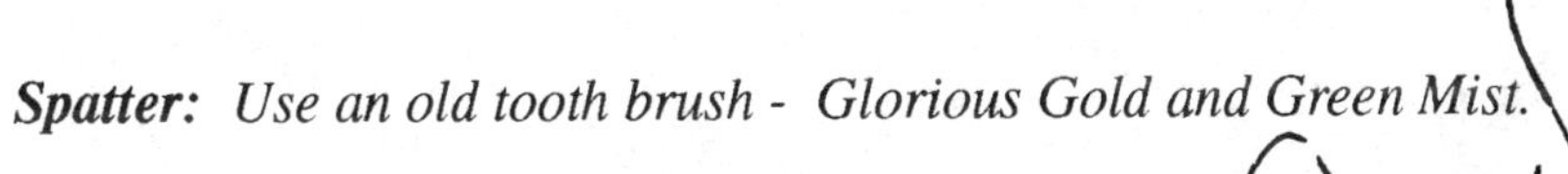

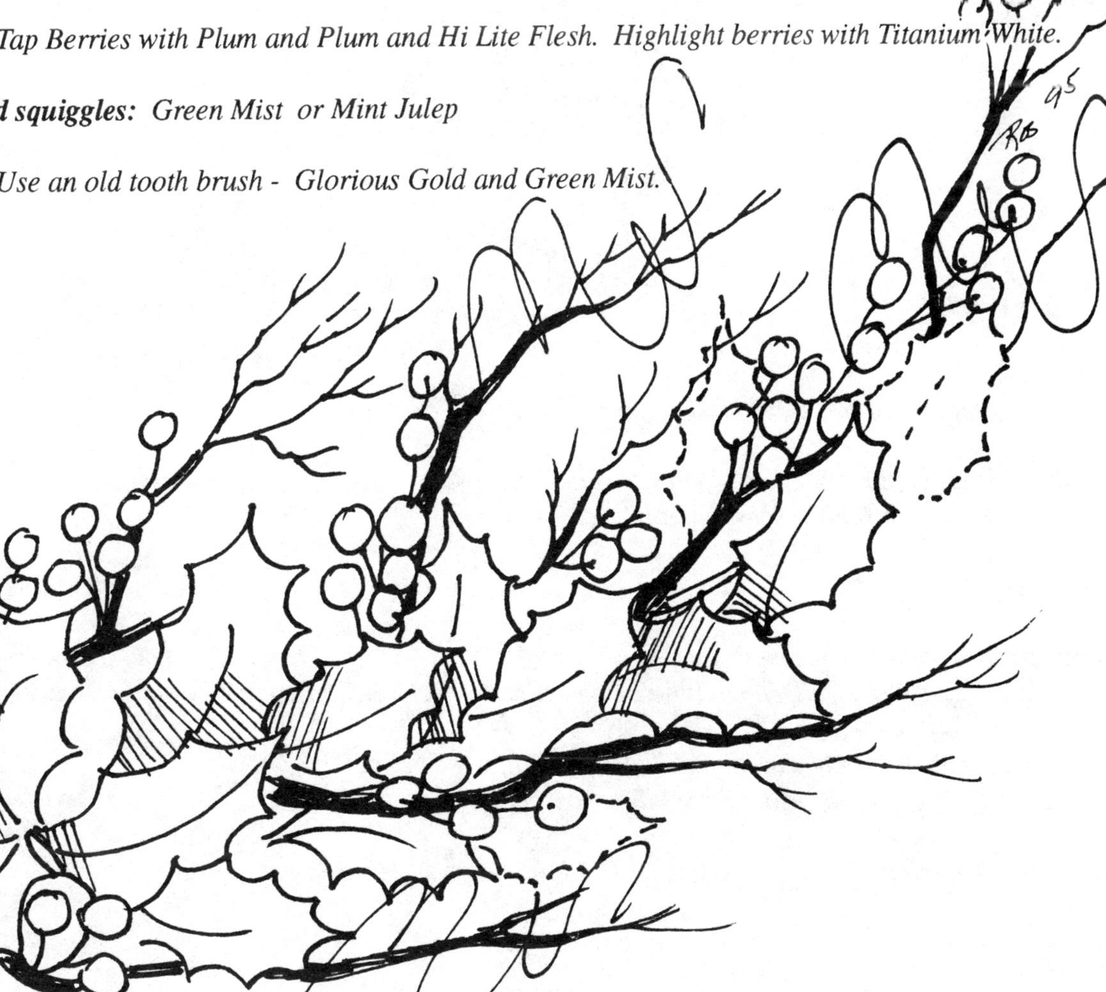

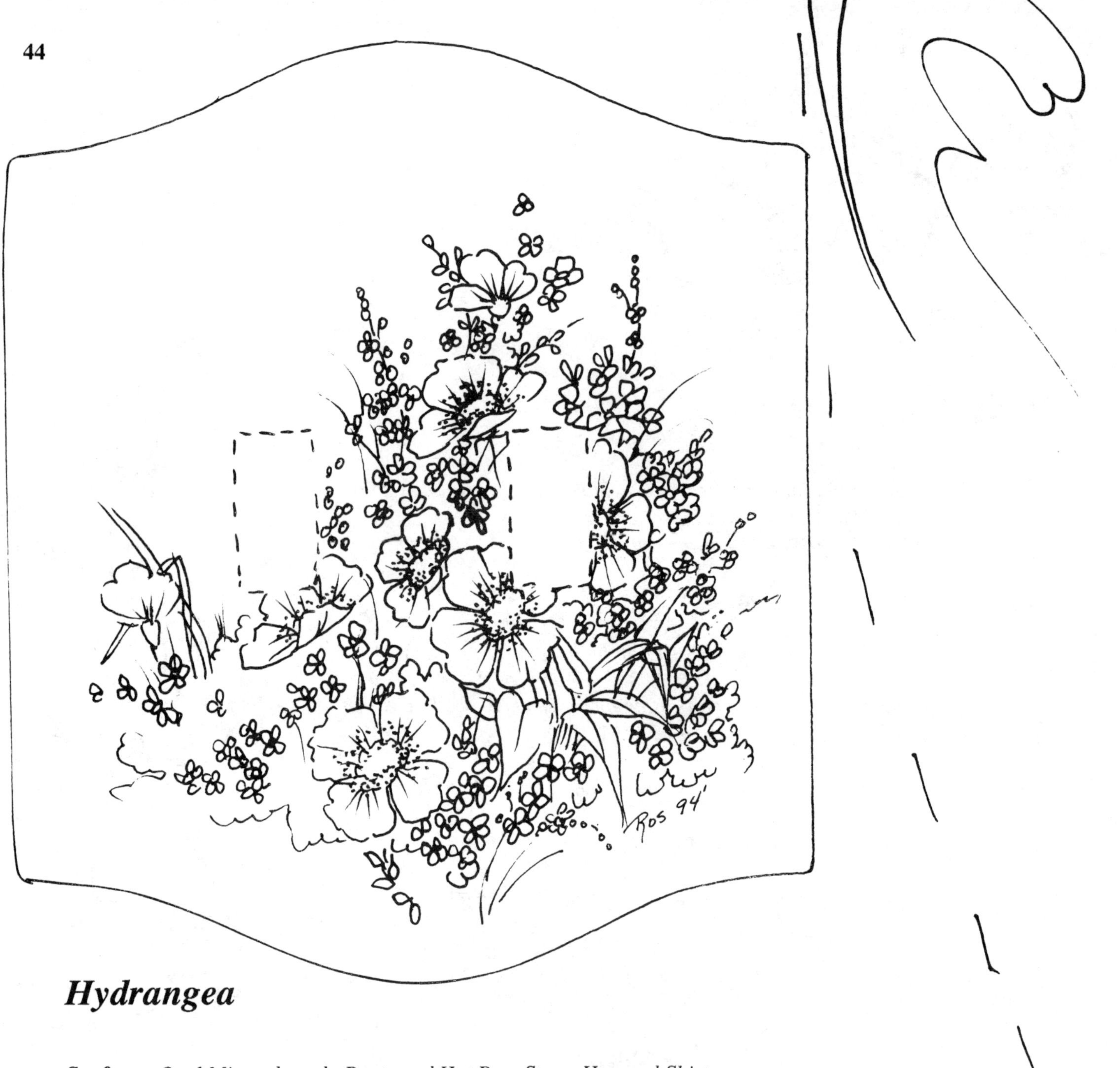

Hydrangea

Surface: *Oval Mirror board, Bentwood Hat Box, Straw Hat, and Shirt*

Paint: *DecoArt Americana Acrylic - Bentwood Hat Box, Oval Mirror Board, Straw Hat*
DecoArt So Soft Fabric Acrylic - Shirt

Leaves: *Base with Avocado. Shade with Evergreen. Highlight with Olive Green or Cadmium Yellow and White.*

Hydrangeas: *Base with Dioxazine Purple, Lavender and Orchid. Paint three and four petal flowers with White with base colors and White with Salem Blue. Centers are Olive Green. Refer to flower worksheets.*

Ribbons: *Base ribbon with Salem Blue. Shade with Teal Green and highlight with White.*
Note: Adjust the colors when using So Soft Fabric Acrylic.

Spatter: *Use an old tooth brush with Glorious Gold. Always test on scrap paper first..*

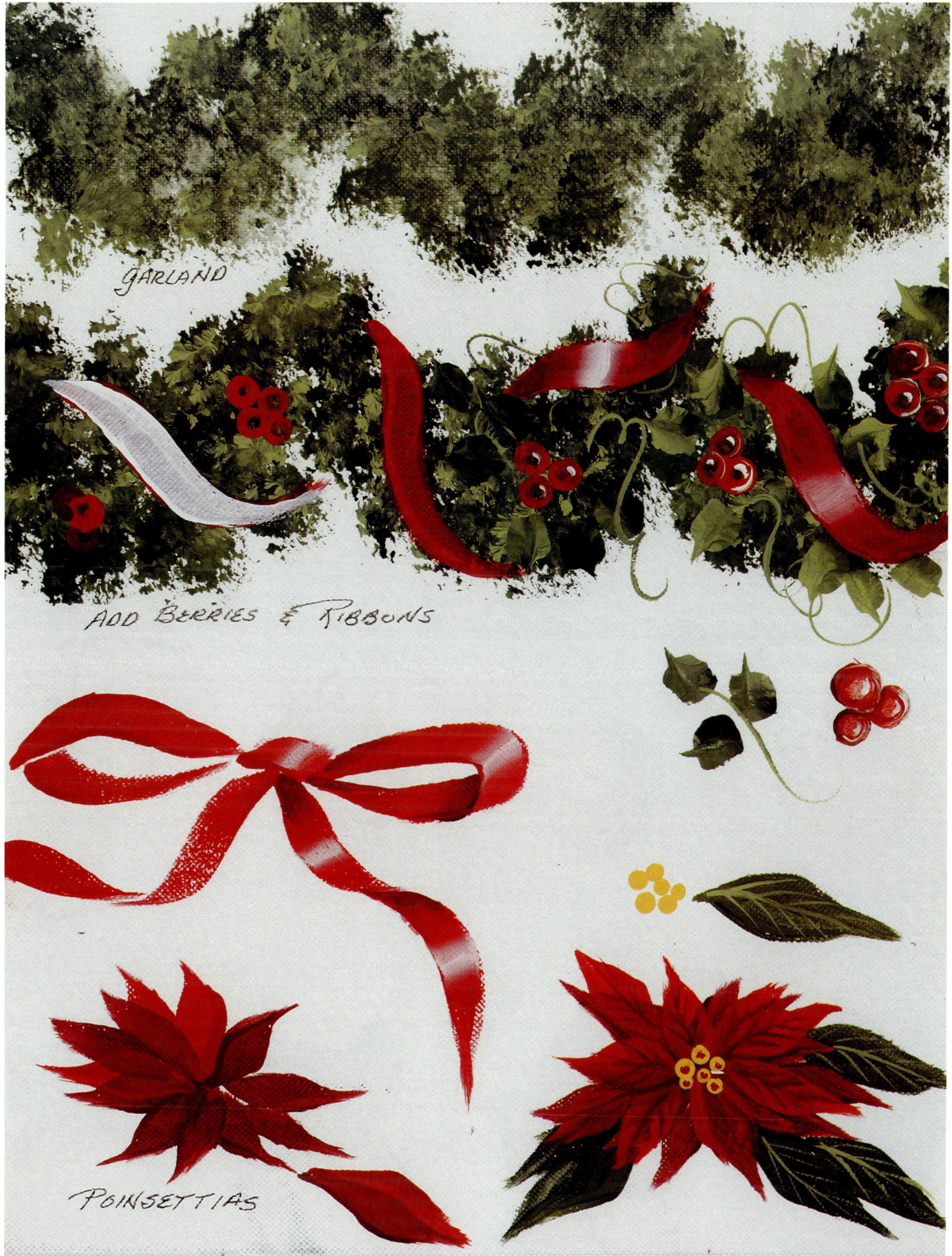
GARLAND
ADD BERRIES & RIBBONS
POINSETTIAS

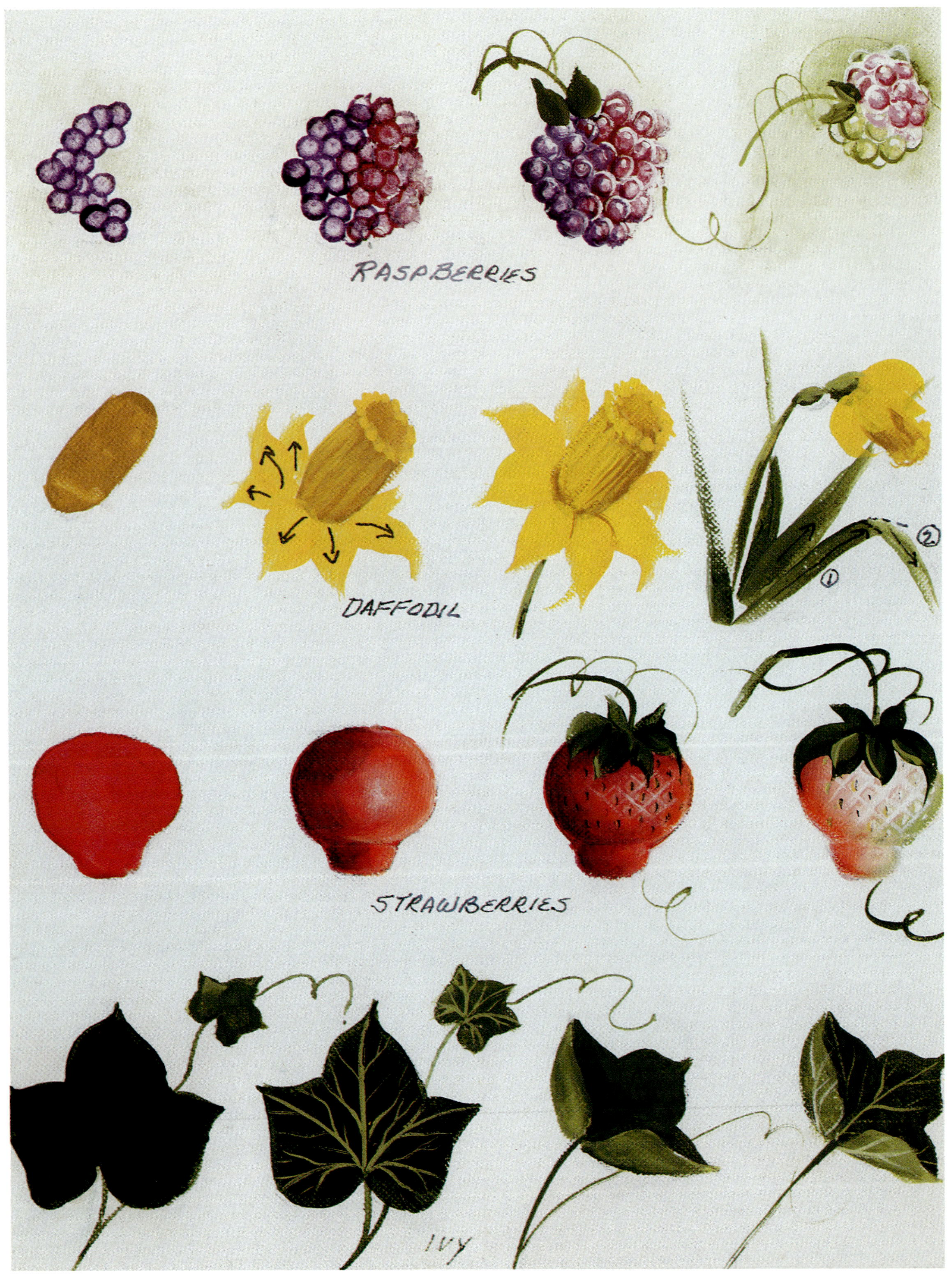

RASPBERRIES
DAFFODIL
①
②
STRAWBERRIES
IVY

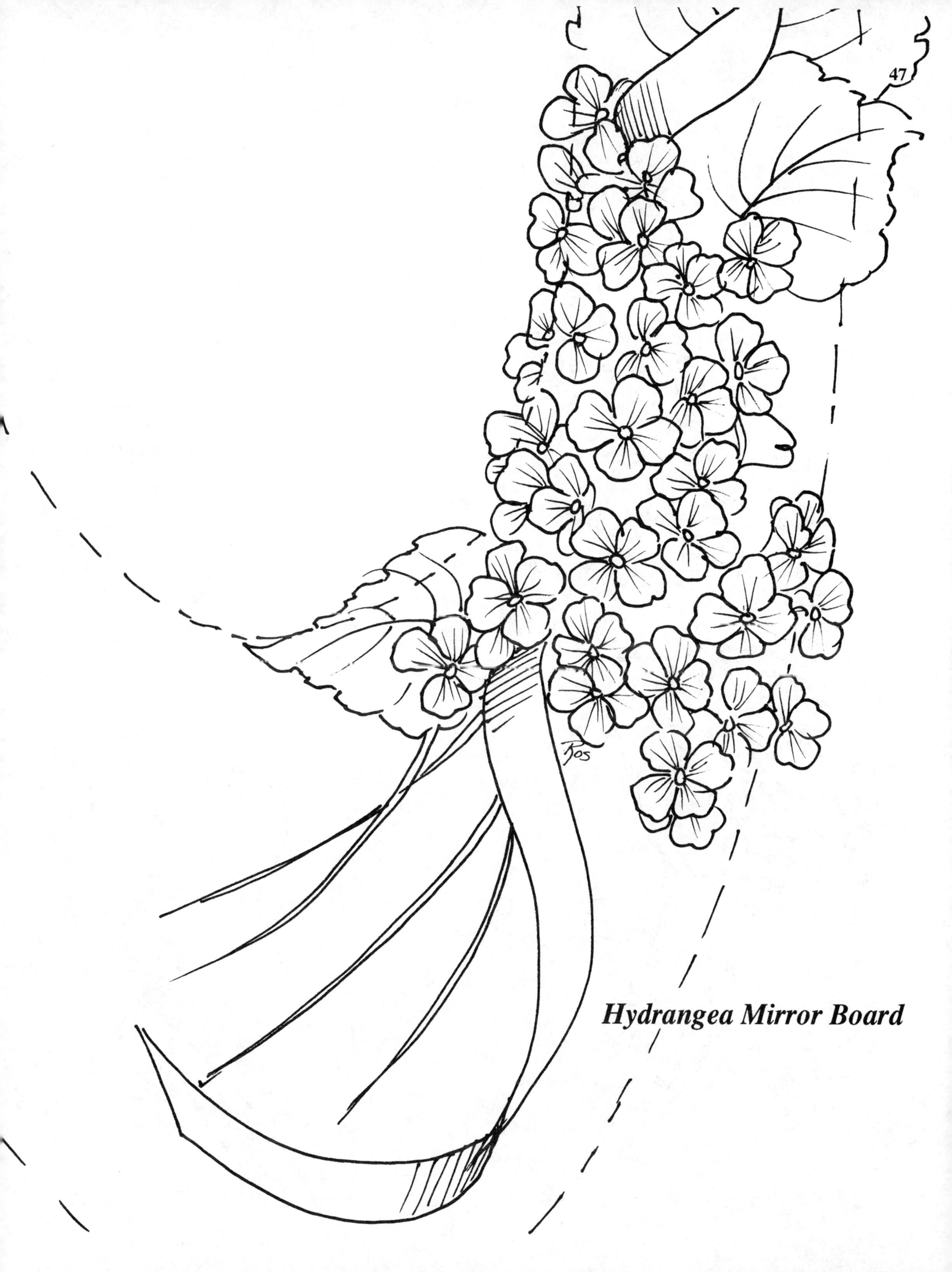

Hydrangea Mirror Board

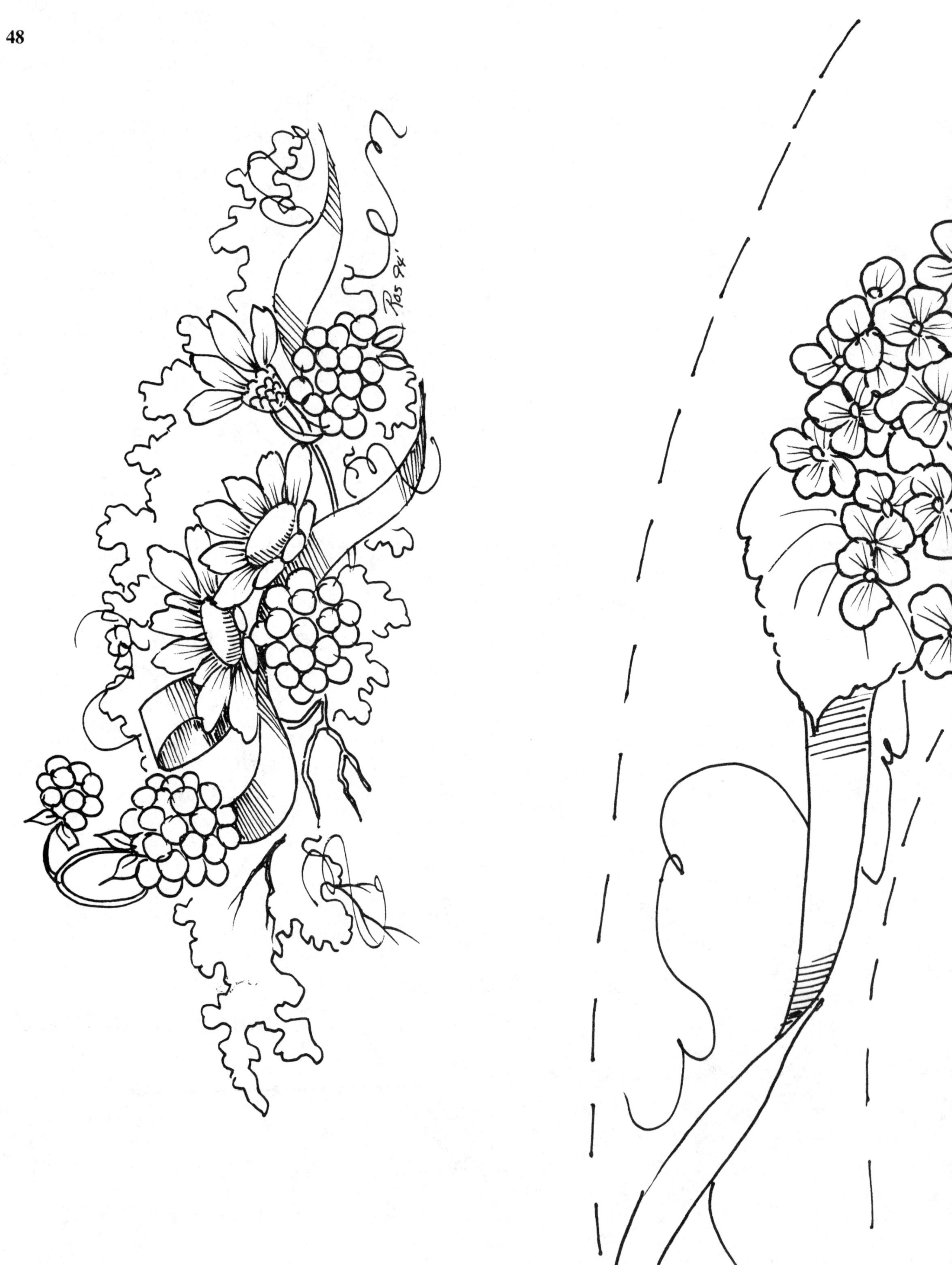

Hydrangea Mirror Board *Avaliable from Stan Brown's Arts and Crafts*

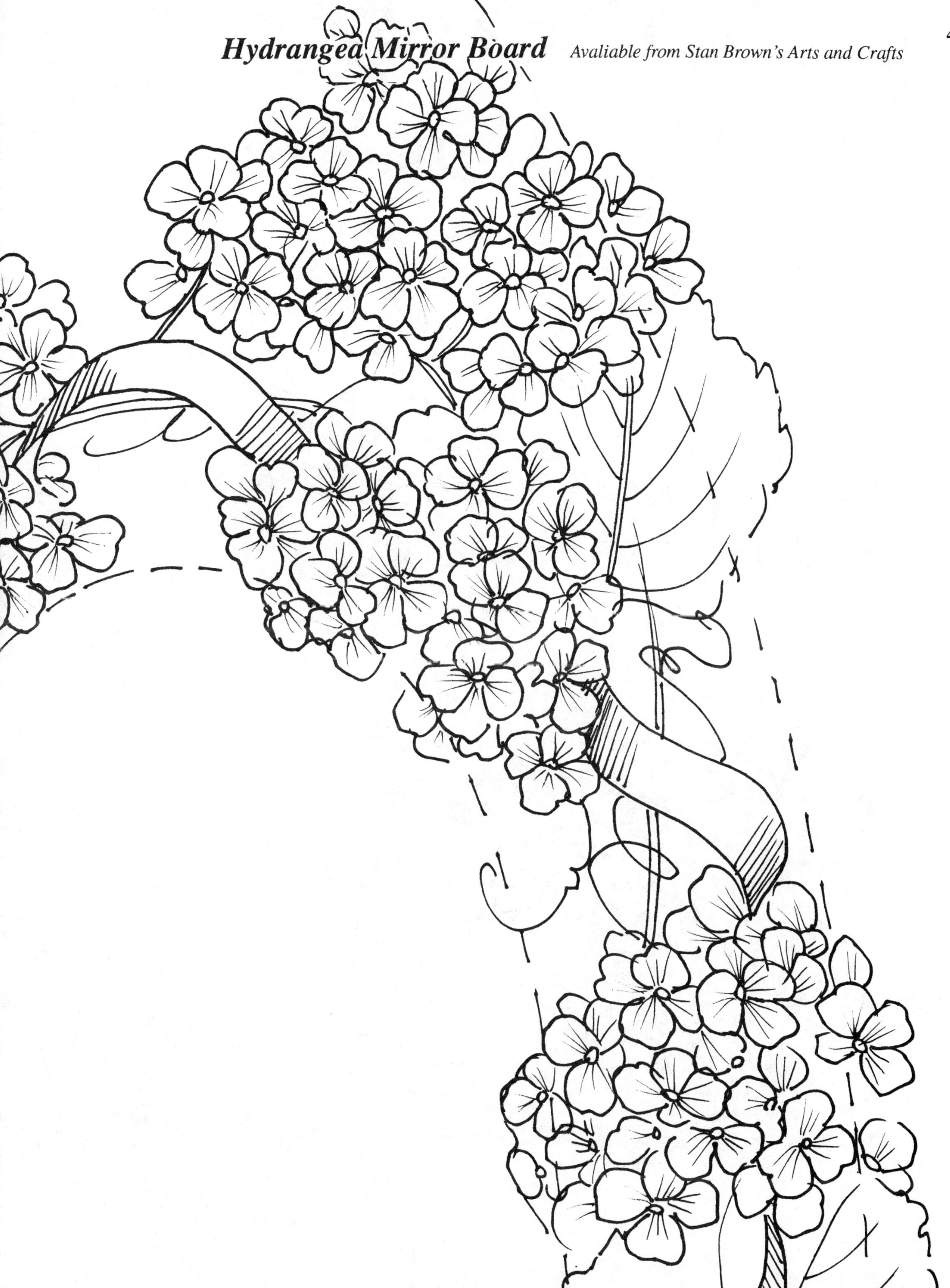

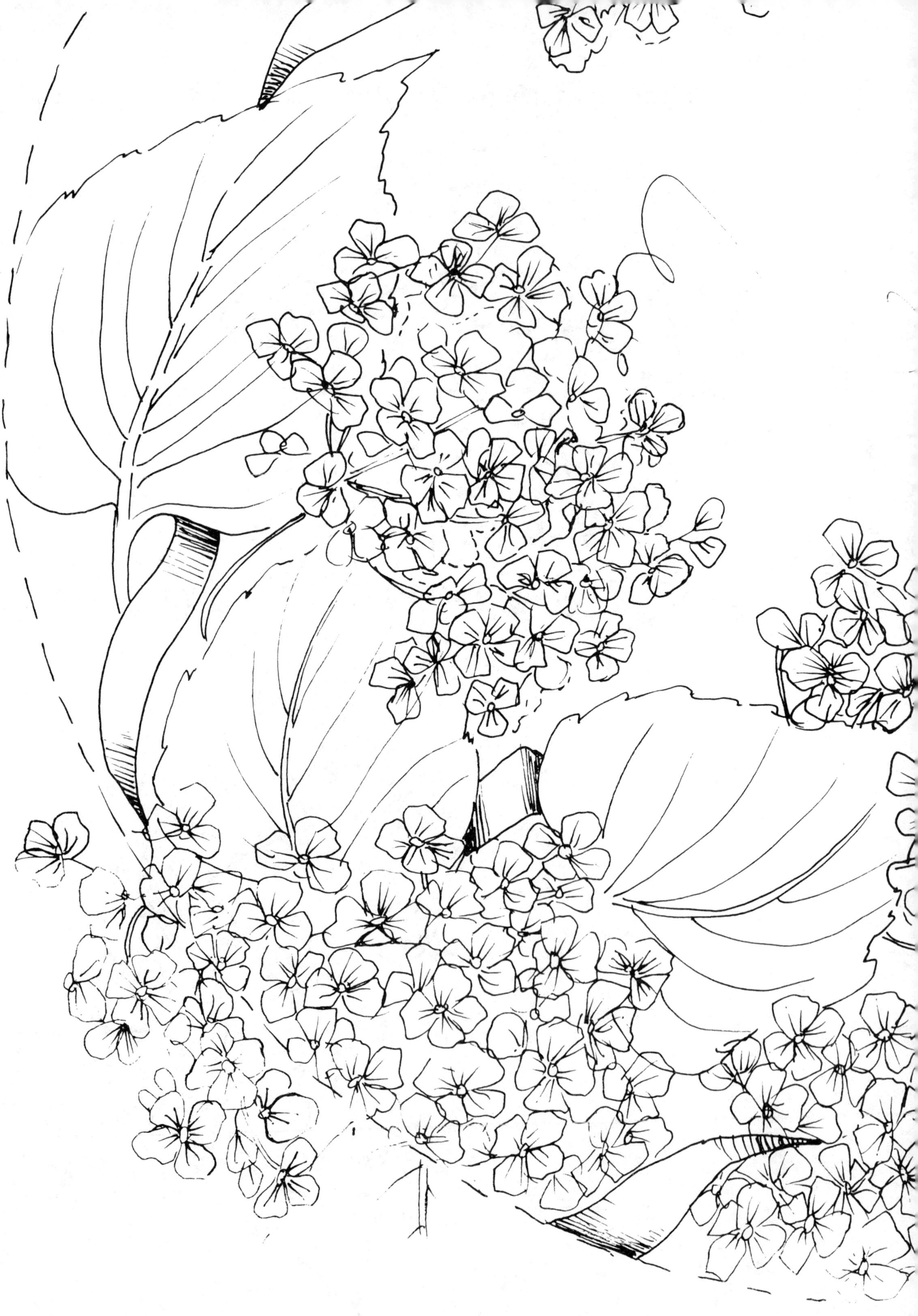

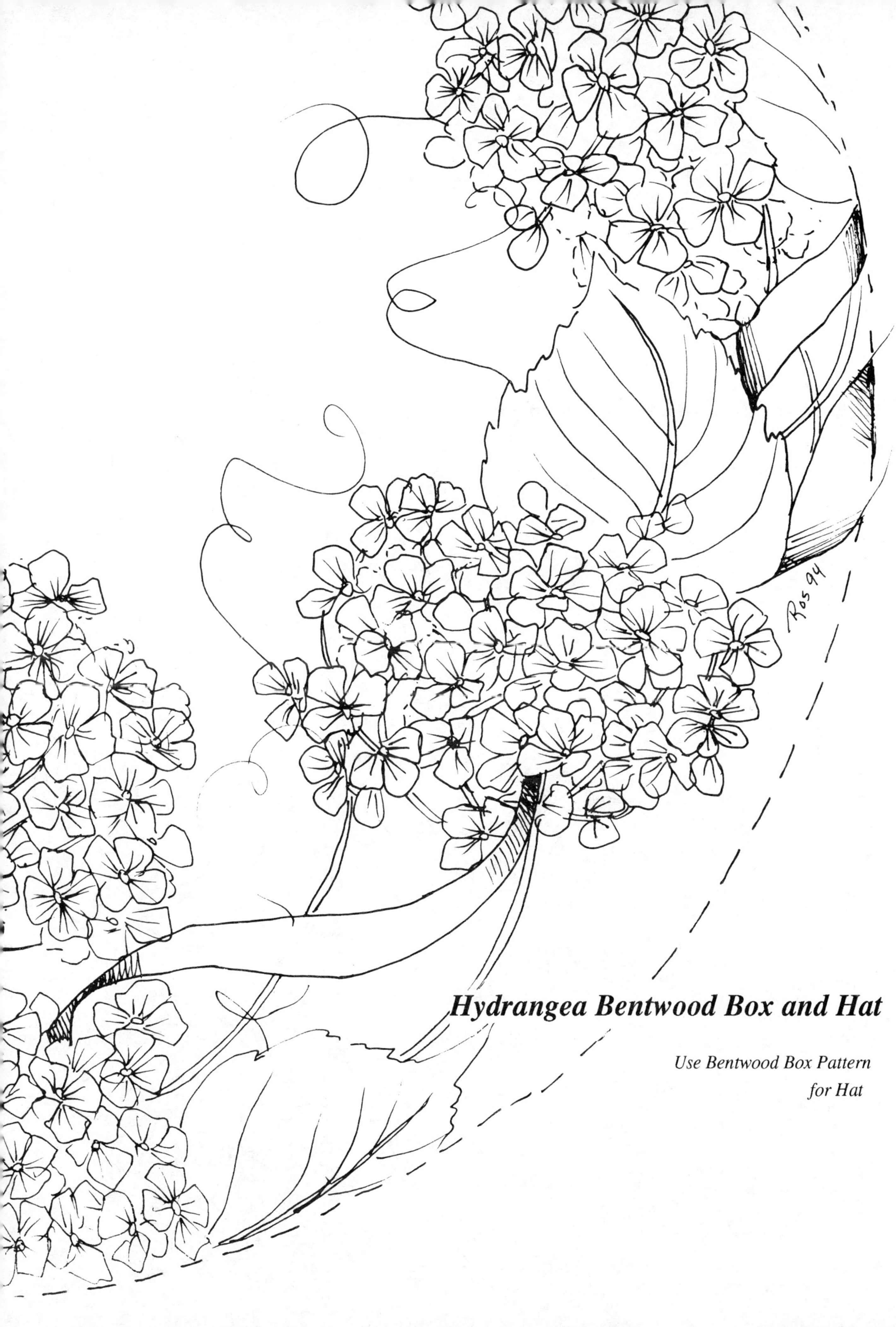

Ros 94

Hydrangea Bentwood Box and Hat

Use Bentwood Box Pattern for Hat

Hydrangea Bentwood Box and Hat

Side of Hydrangea Hat Box

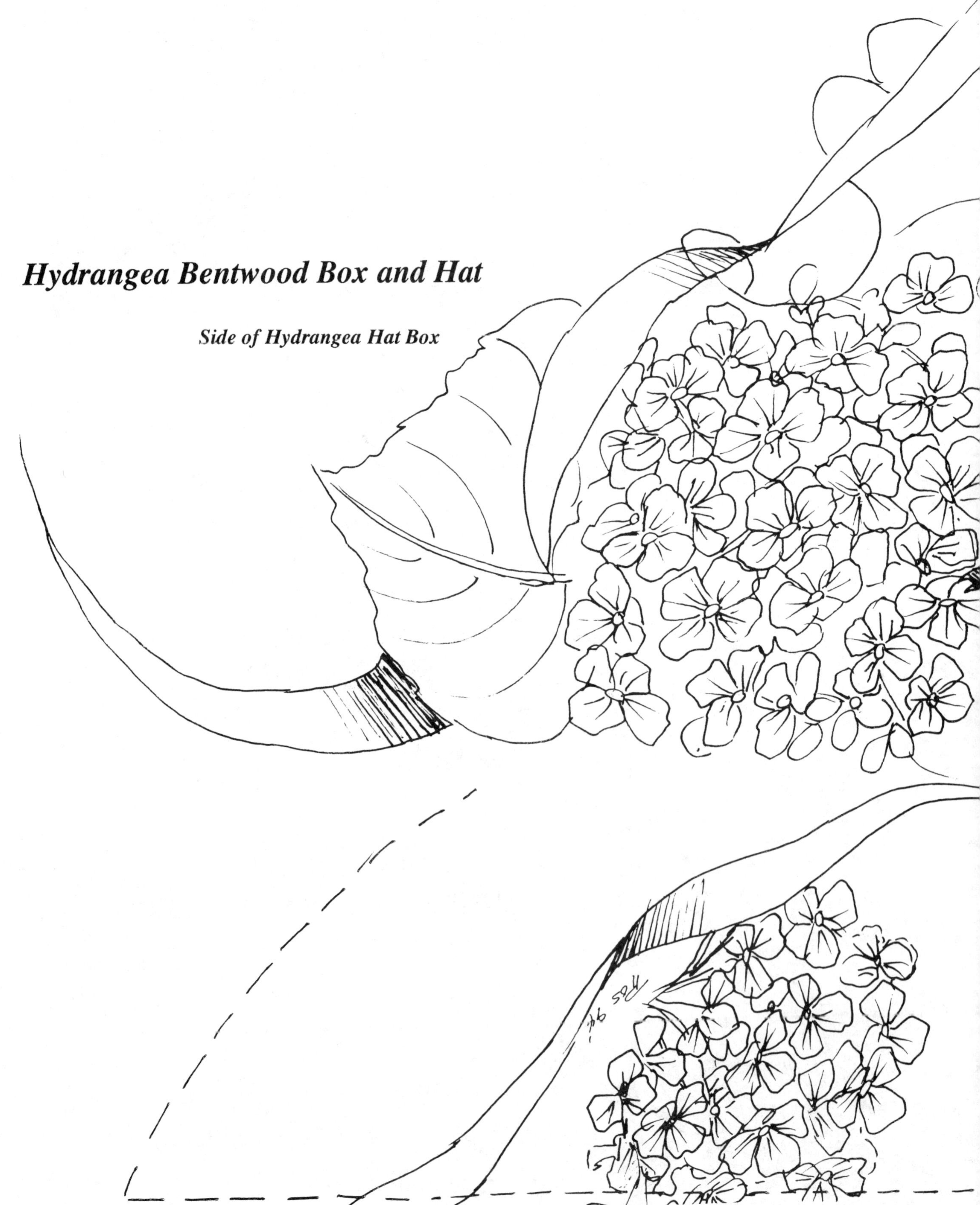

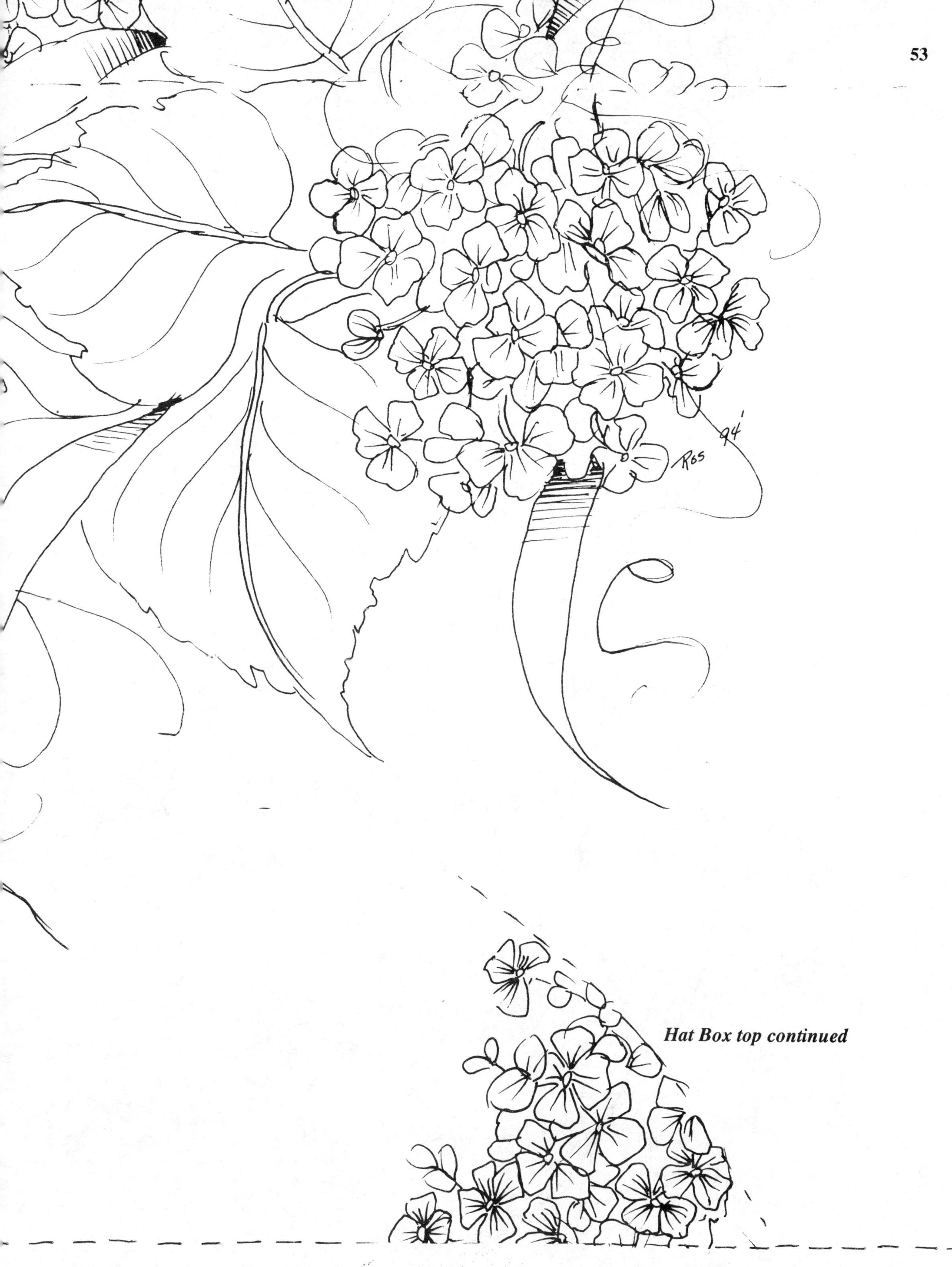

Hat Box top continued

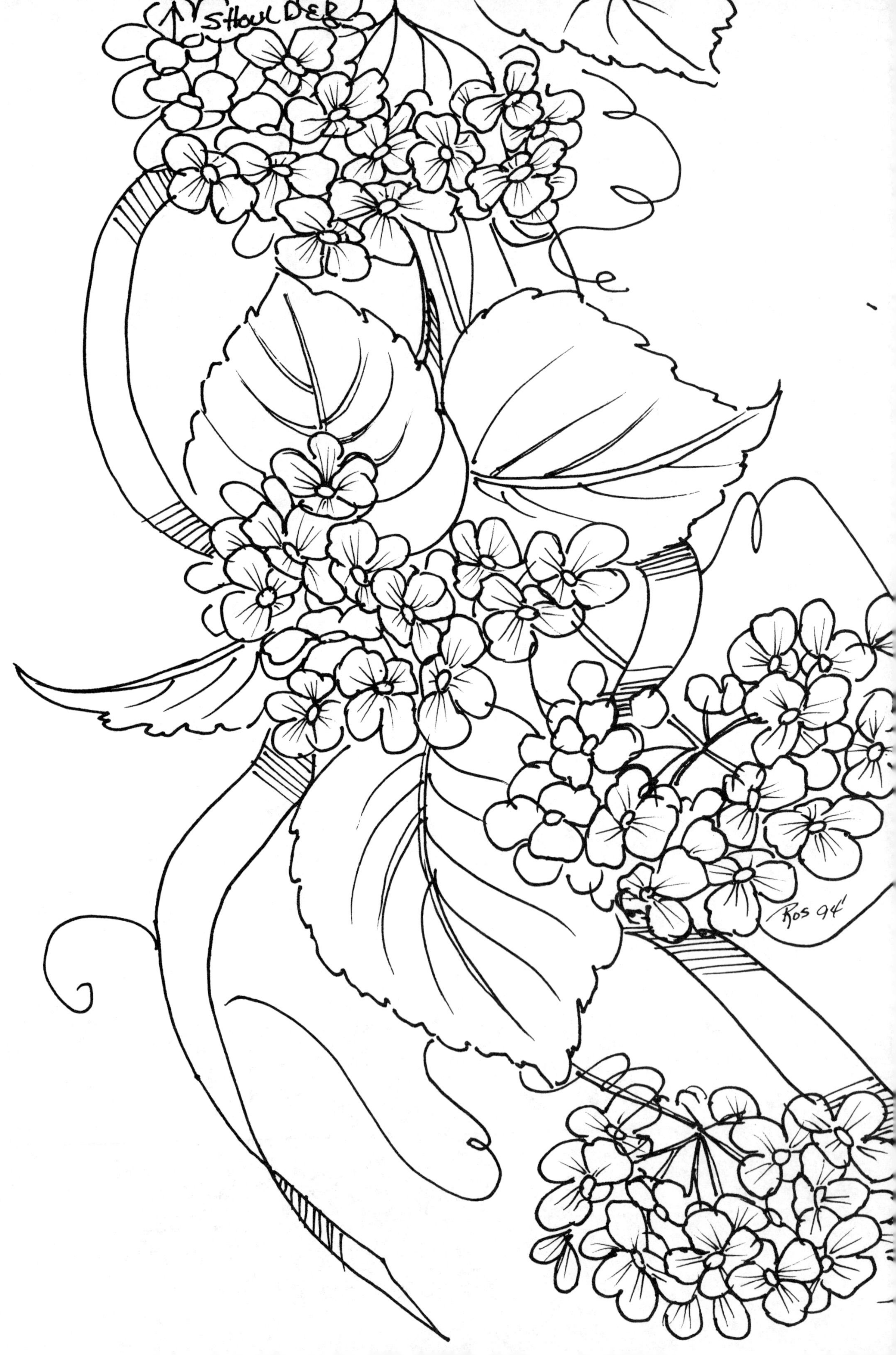
SHOULDER
Ros 94'

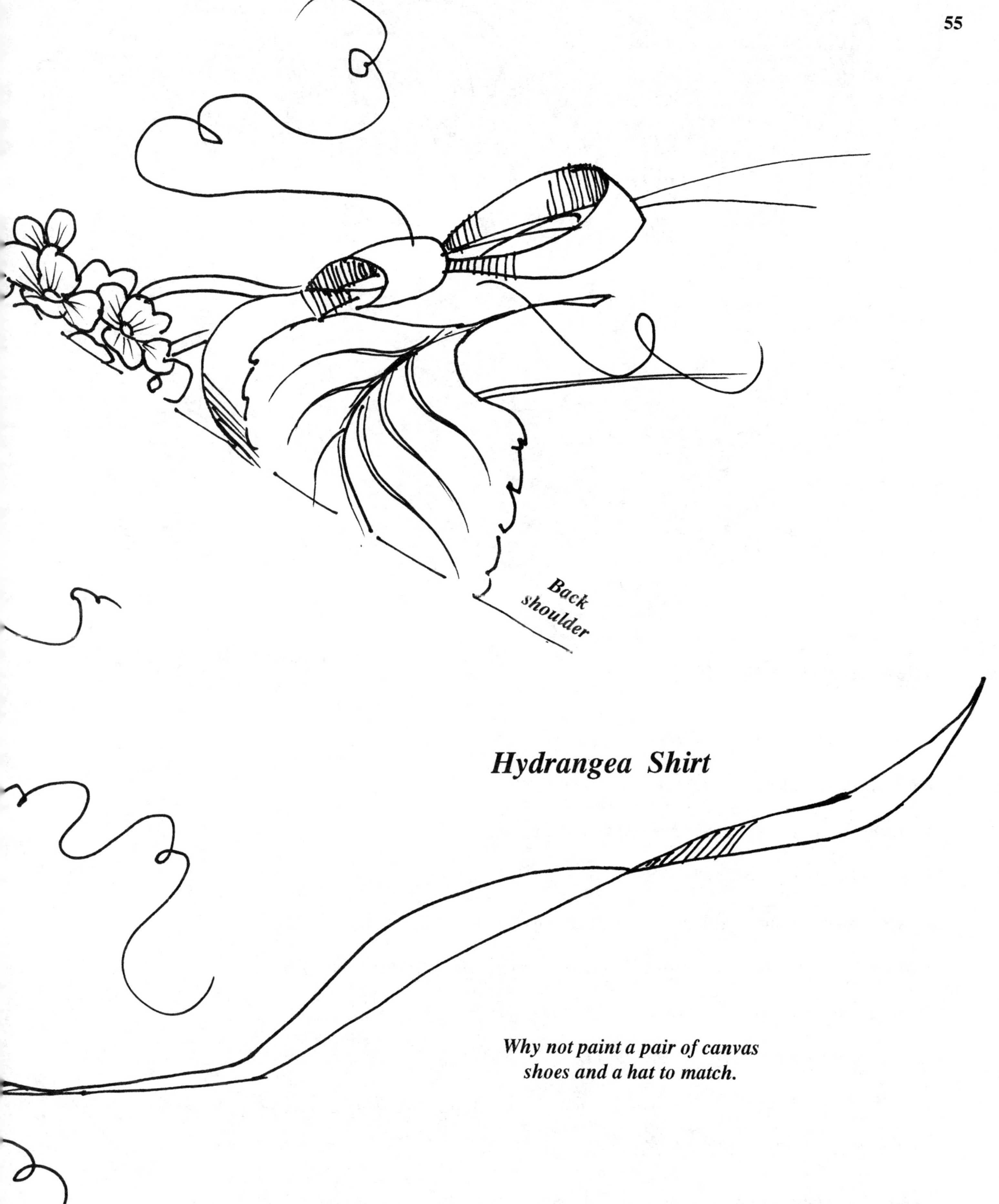

Hydrangea Shirt

Why not paint a pair of canvas shoes and a hat to match.

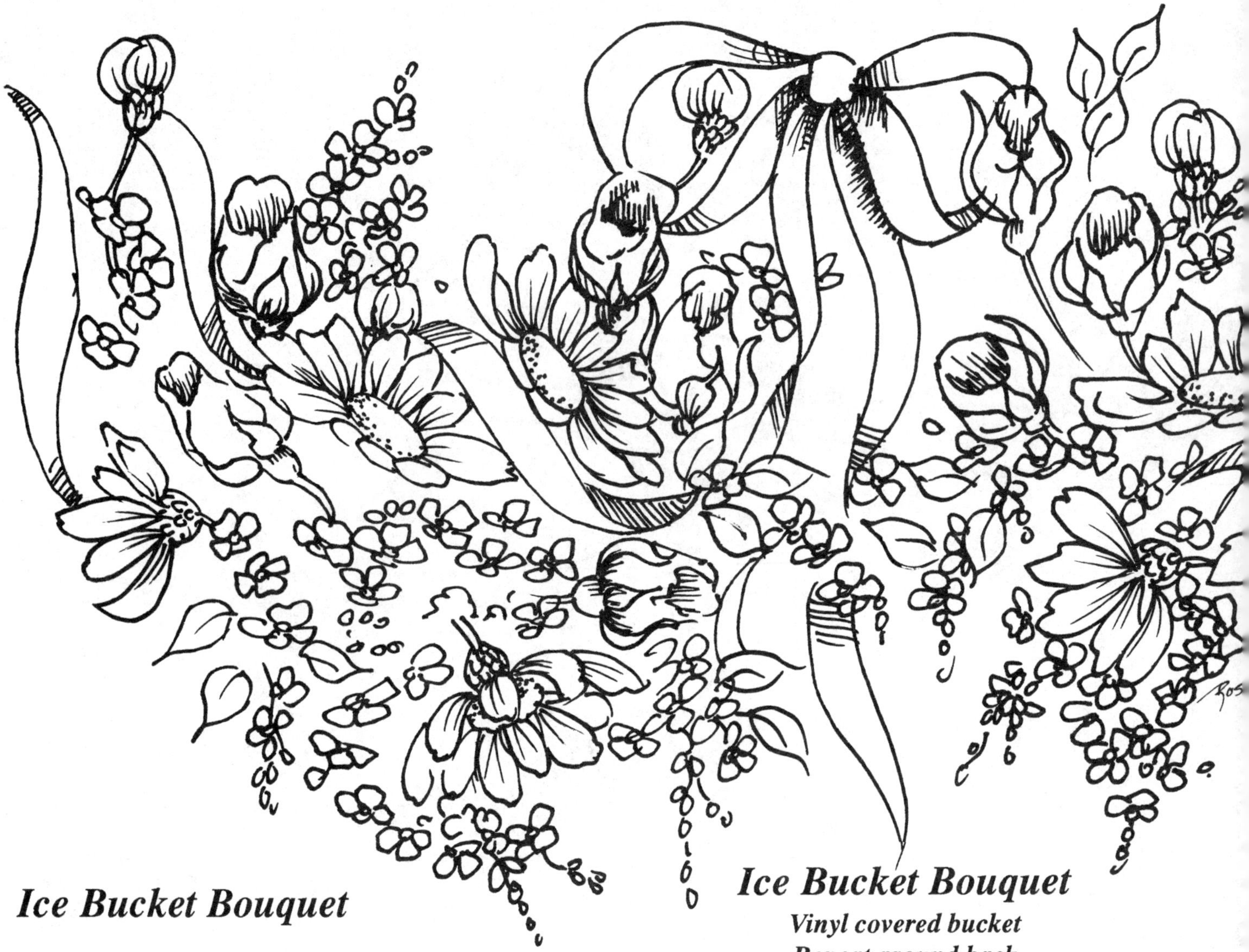

Ice Bucket Bouquet

Ice Bucket Bouquet
Vinyl covered bucket
Repeat around back

Surface: *Vinyl Covered Ice Bucket*

Paint: *DecoArt Americana Acrylic*

Basecoat: *Sand vinyl lightly and base with two coats of acrylic of your choice.*

Foliage: *Evergreen, Avocado, and Olive Green.*

Daises: *Titanium White, Paint centers with Cadmium Yellow and shade with Burnt Sienna..*

Ribbons: *Baby Blue, shade with Williamsburg Blue and highlight with Titanium White.*

Rosebud: *Base with Napa Red and Baby Pink. Highlight with Baby Pink and Titanium White.*

Calyxes Stems and Squiggles: *Avocado and Olive Green.*

Filler Flowers: *Dioxazine Purple and Dioxazine Purple and Titanium White.*

Spatter: *Glorious Gold and Baby Blue.*

Varnish: *J.W. Right Step Varnish several coats - always read directions on the label.*

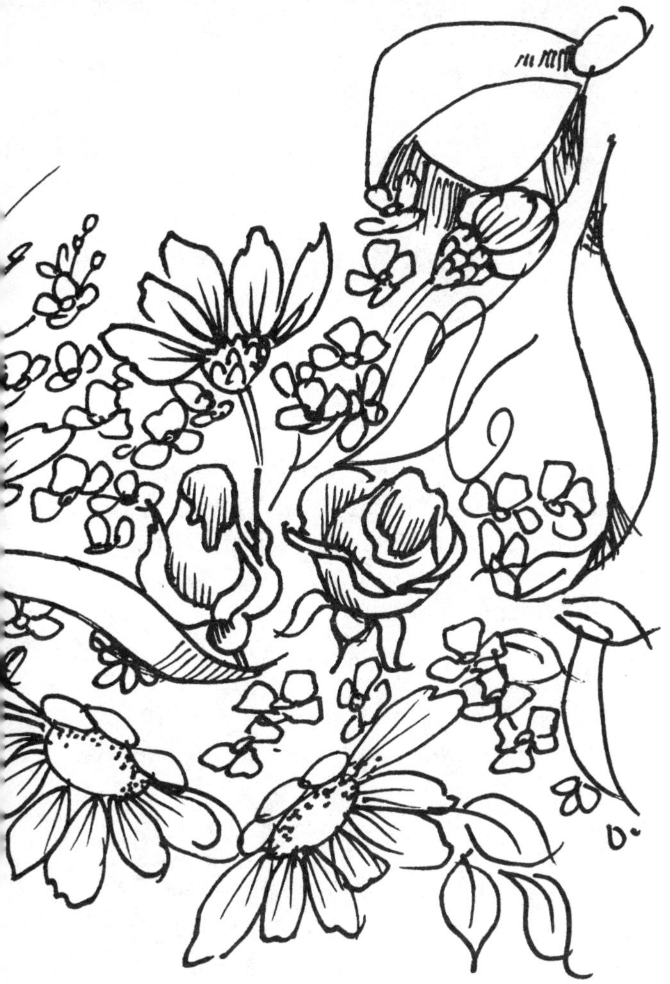

Puffed Heart Pins
Refer to step by steps in front of book.

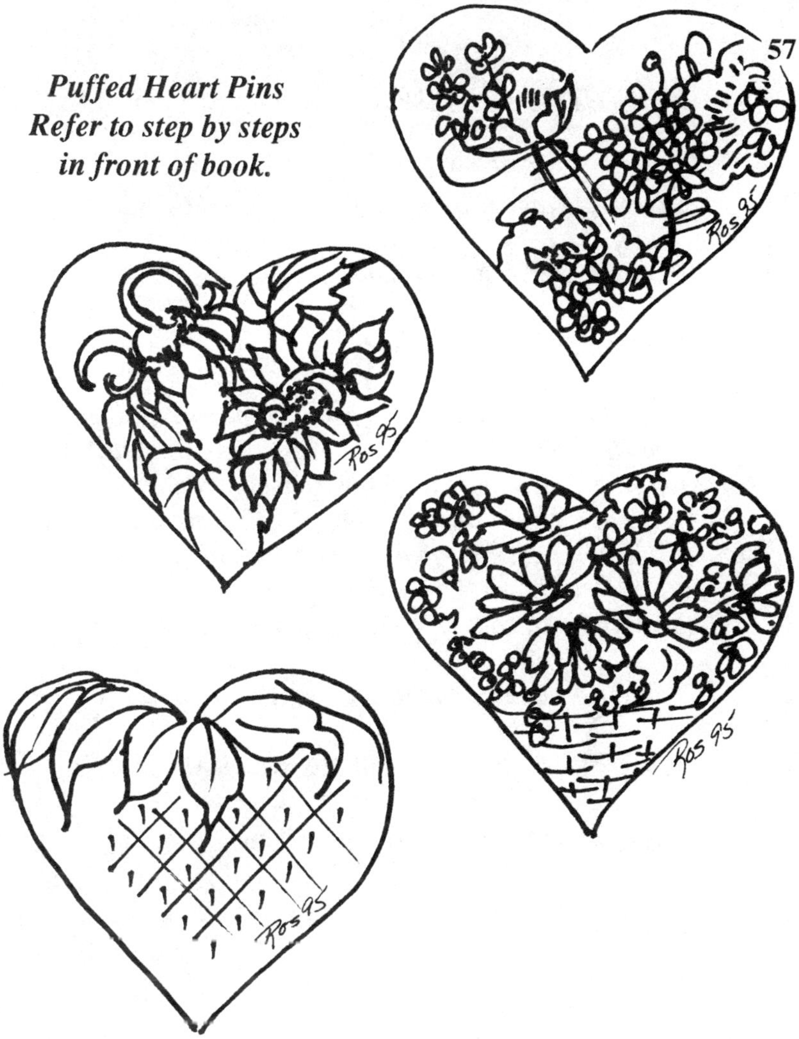

Ice Bucket Bouquet

Might be a great way to revive that old ice bucket sitting on your top shelf. Try on a simple Styrofoam ice bucket.. Tie with a satin bow for a quick gift.

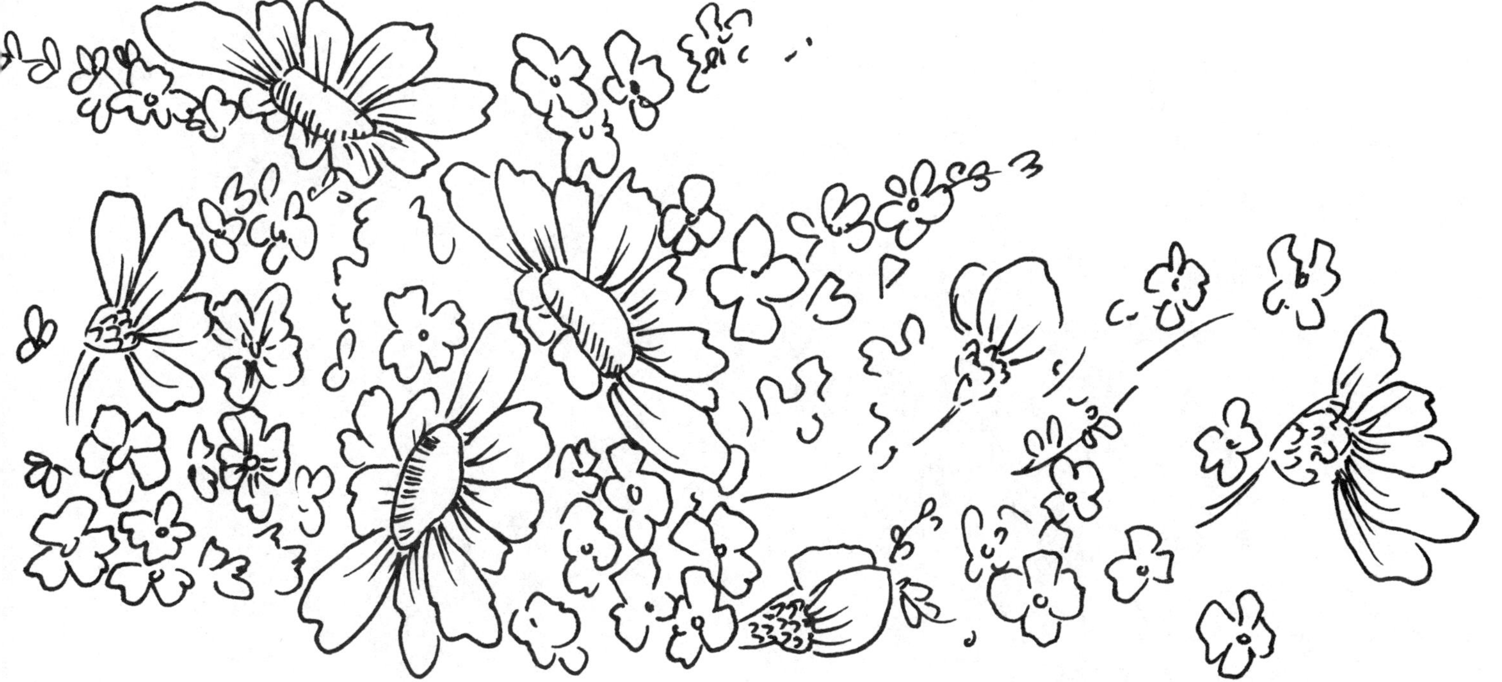

Wisteria Garden

Surface: *Lattice Towel Rack, Allan Wood Crafts, 3020 Dogwood Lane, Sapulpa, Ok 74066*

Paint: *DecoArt Americana Acrylic*

Basecoat: *J.W. White Lightning*

Scene through the Lattice Arbor: *Tape up the inner side of the arbor with masking tape. Sky is Baby Blue and Baby Blue with White. Extend your paint with Blush and Blend to make it easier to blend colors. Tap foliage on top with Jade, Avocado, Baby Blue and White. Paint tree trunks with Mississippi Mud. Re-highlight foliage with Olive Green and Olive Green with White. Paint water with sky colors using Blush and Blend. Pull down reflections with your tree colors and blend across. Flip up grass with Avocado. Let dry.*

Mist: *Paint a coat of White Lightning over the scene. Allow to dry. Remove masking tape.*

Foliage on Lattice Arbor: *Evergreen, Avocado and Olive Green. Spill some foliage over the edge the board.*

Vines: *Dark Chocolate and Mississippi Mud.*

Wisteria: *Dioxazine Purple with White.*

Leaves and stems: *Avocado and Olive Green*

Wisteria

Surfaces: *Ceramic Soap Dish, Bathroom Glass, and Plastic Tissue Box*

Paint: *DecoArt Ultra Gloss Acrylic Enamel*

Leaves: *Avocado*

Branches: *Chocolate and Chocolate with White*

Wisteria: *Purple and Purple with White*

Stems and squiggles: *Avocado*

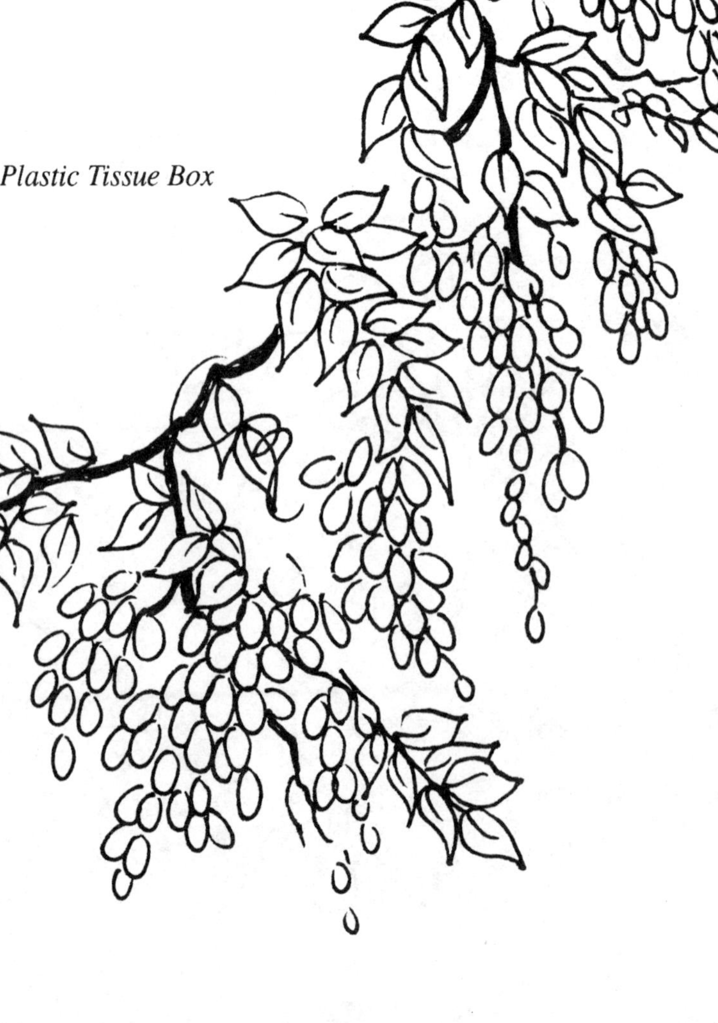

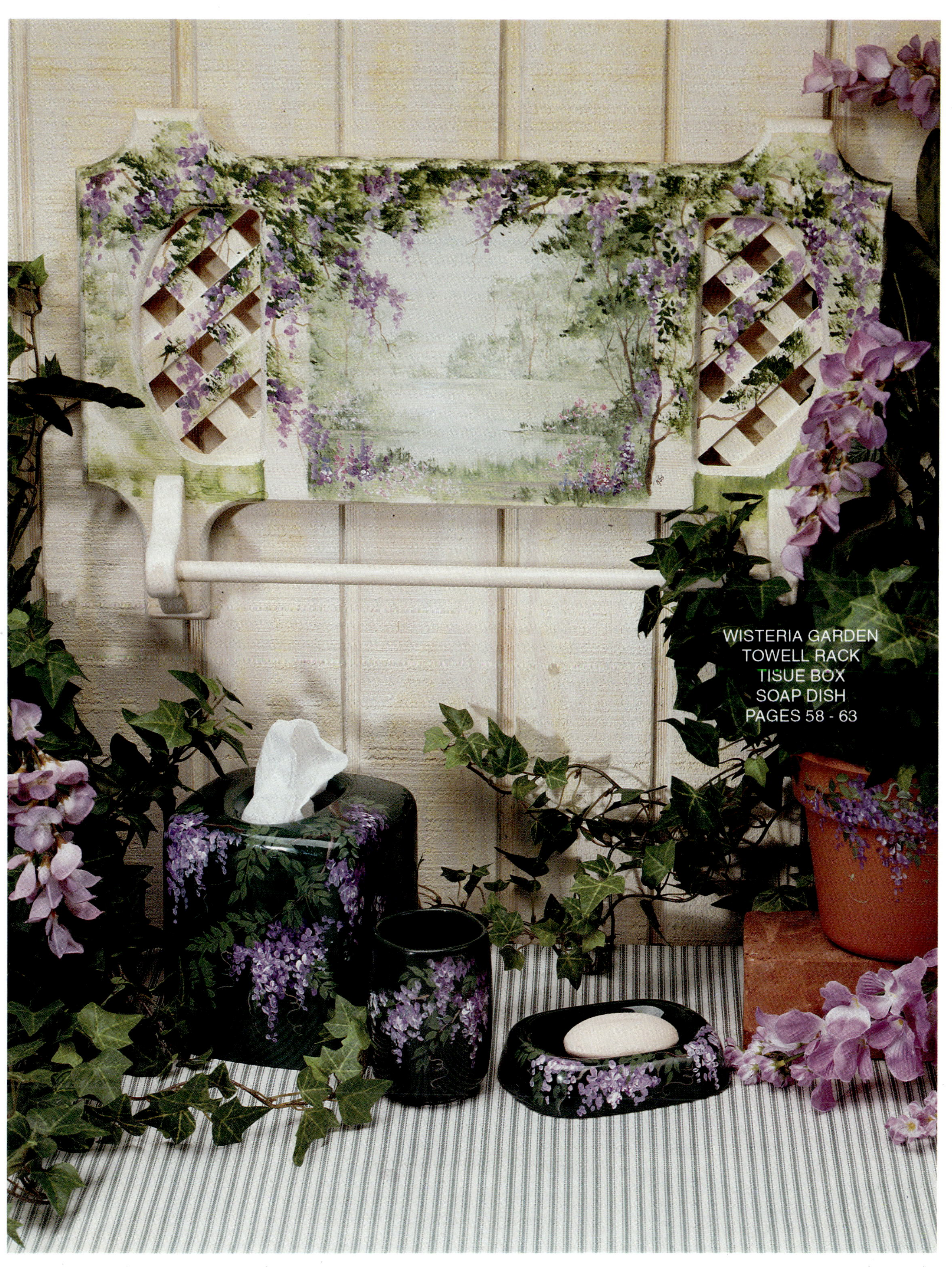

WISTERIA GARDEN
TOWELL RACK
TISUE BOX
SOAP DISH
PAGES 58 - 63

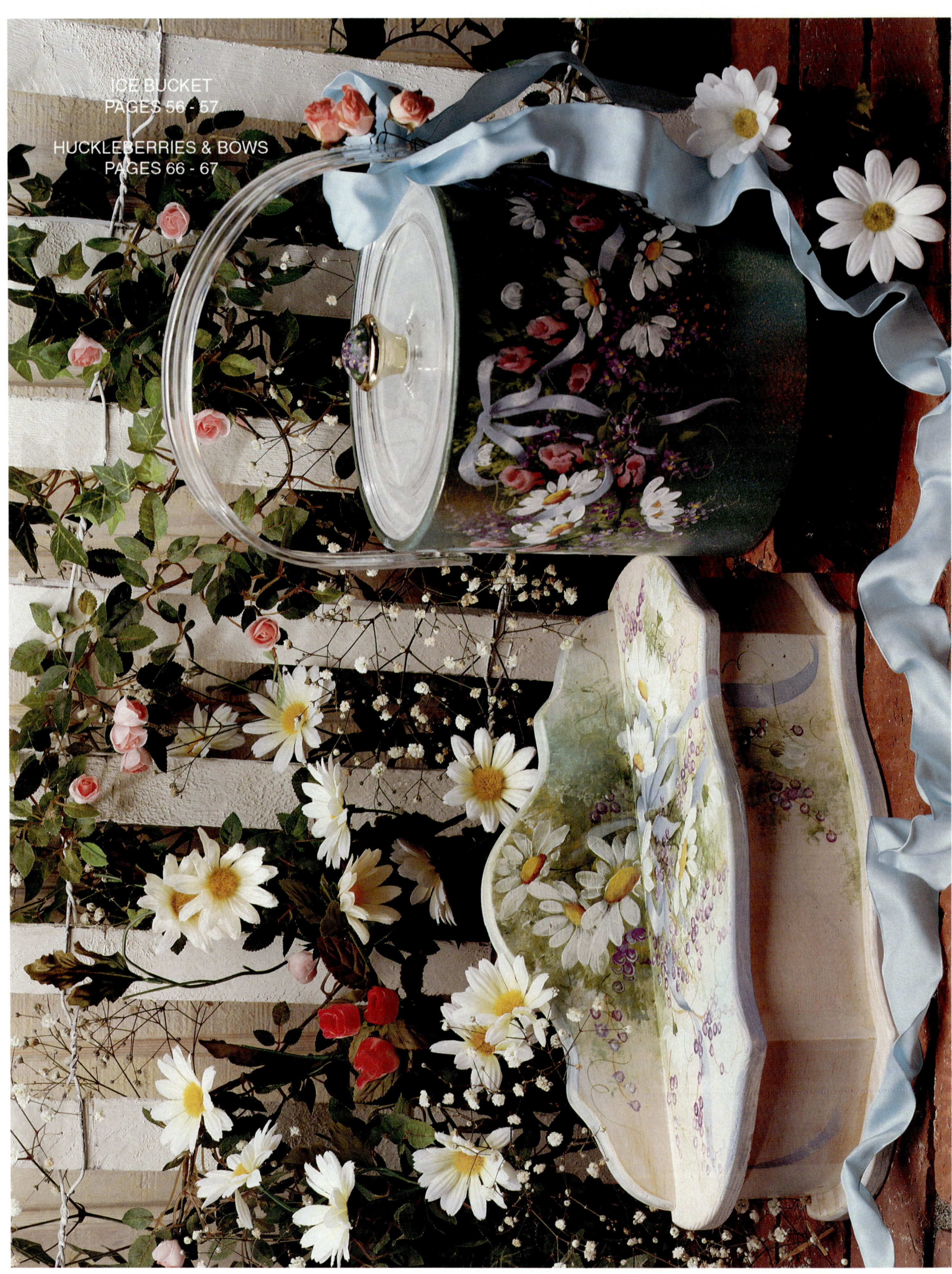

ICE BUCKET
PAGES 56 - 57

HUCKLEBERRIES & BOWS
PAGES 66 - 67

Ros 94'

Wisteria Tissue Box

Ros 94'

Wisteria Soap Dish

SOHr

Wisteria Garden

Towel Rack avaliable from Allen's Wood Crafts

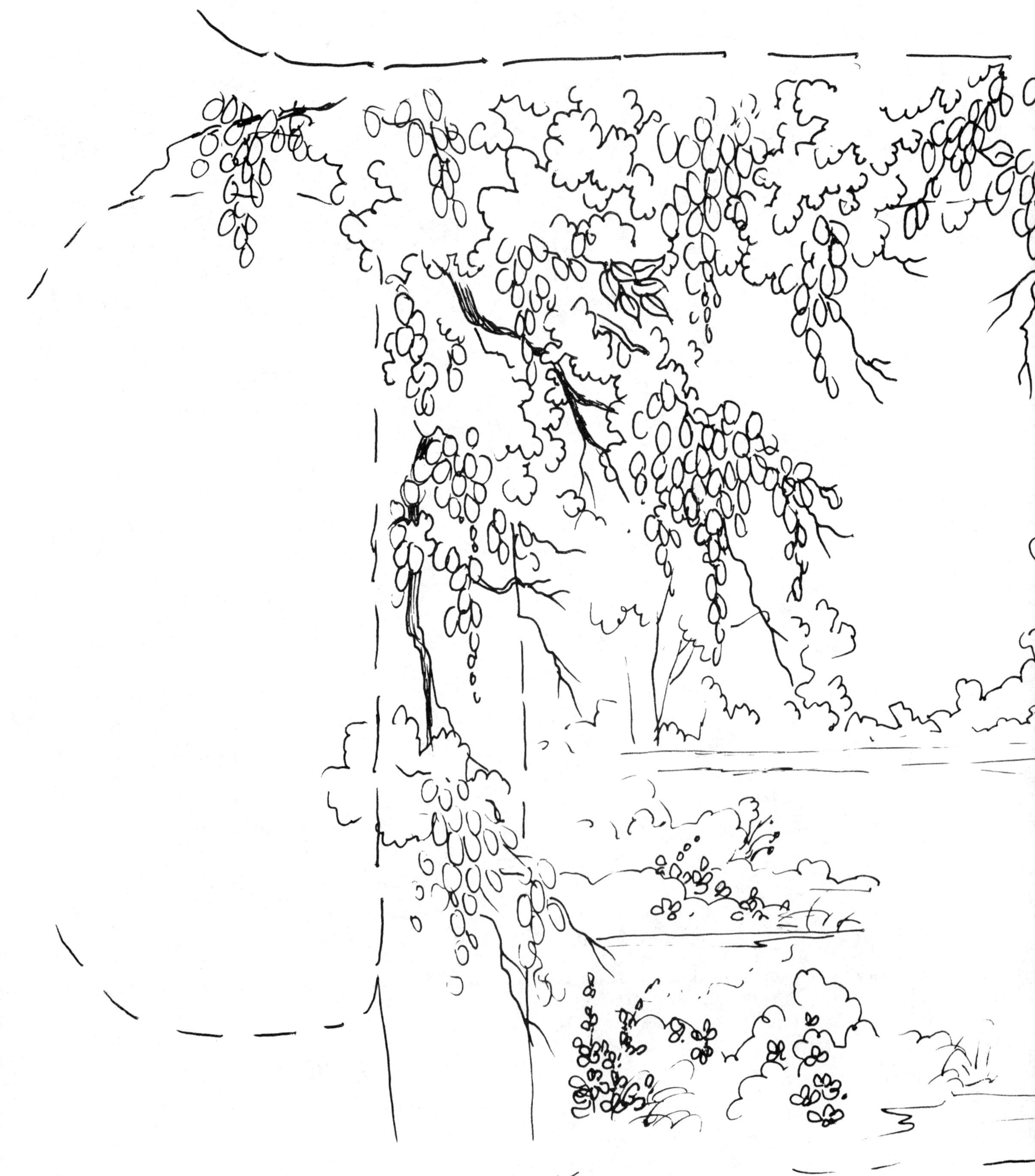

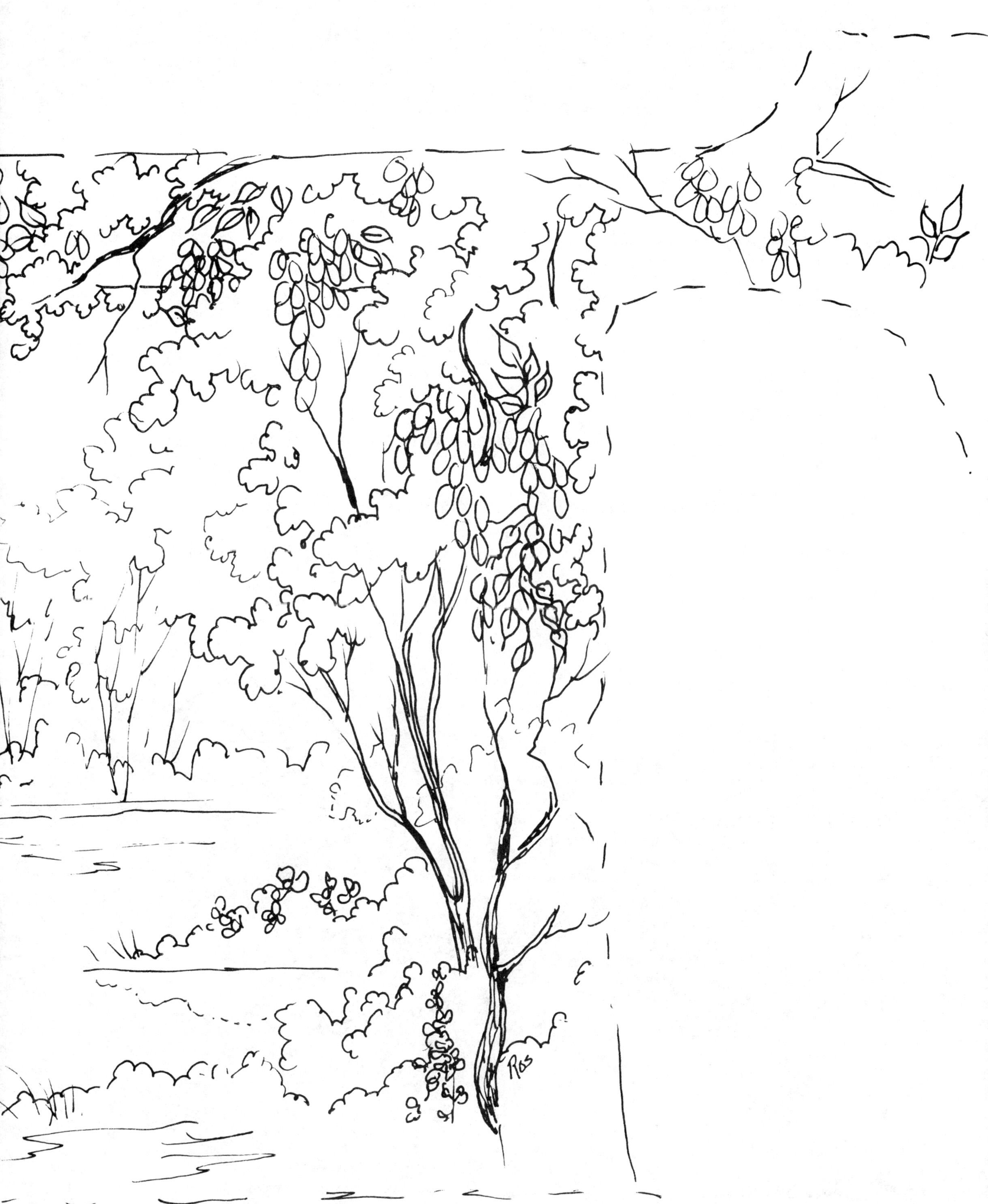
Ros

Ruler

Gran's Daisy Doodles

Surface: *1-1/2 inch Wooden Rulers - Plum Fun , Wooden Plaque*

Paints: *DecoArt Americana Acrylic*

Basecoat: *J. W. White Lightning*

Foliage: *Evergreen, Avocado, and Olive Green - allow to dry and add a few touches of Dioxazine Purple and Titanium White.*

Daises: *Titanium White. Base Centers with Cadmium Yellow and shade with Burnt Sienna..*

Raspberries: *Dioxazine Purple, Red Violet and Red Violet and Titanium White. Highlight with Titanium White.*

Stems, Calyxes, and Squiggles: *Avocado or Olive Green.*

Doodle Board

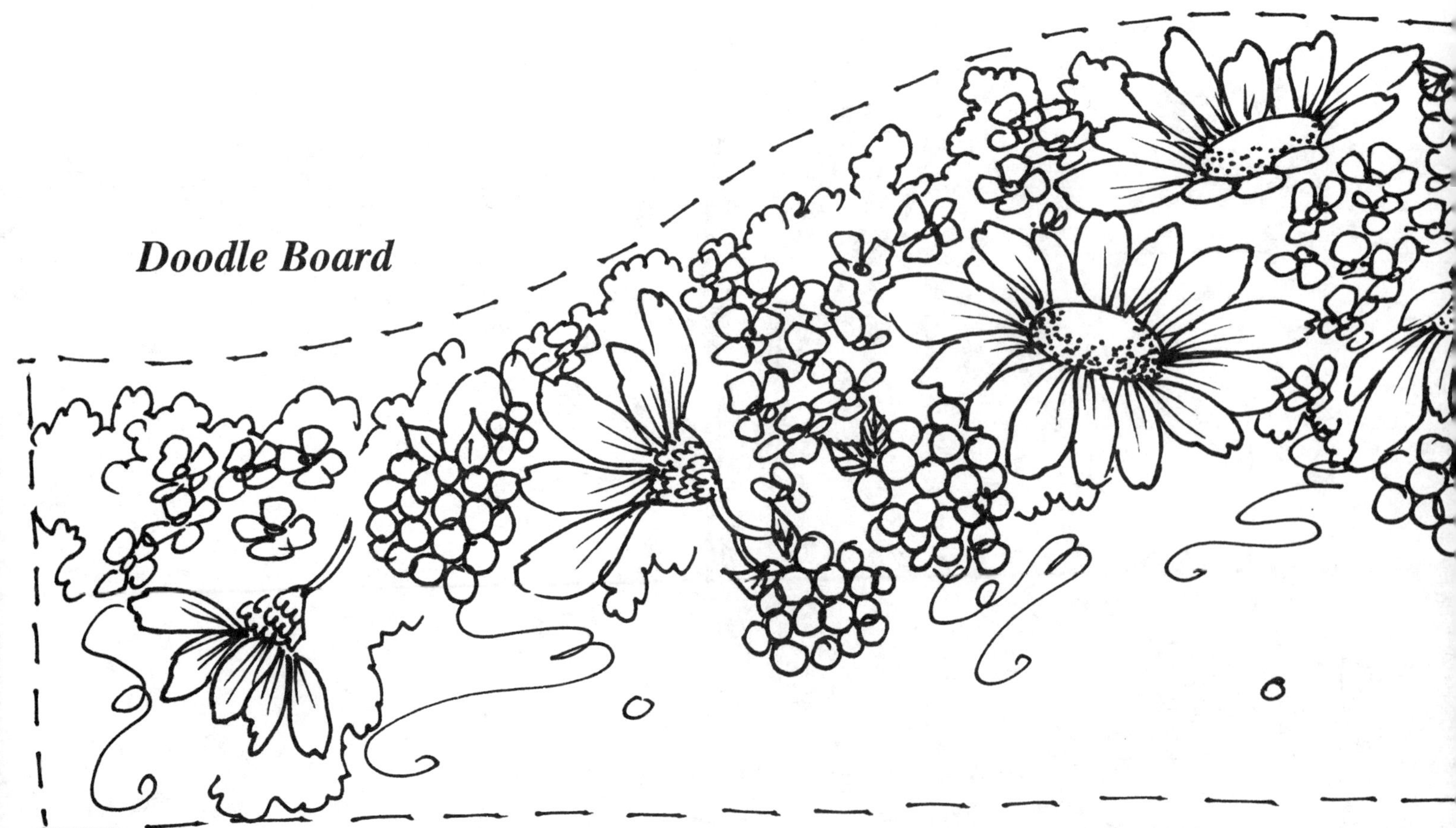

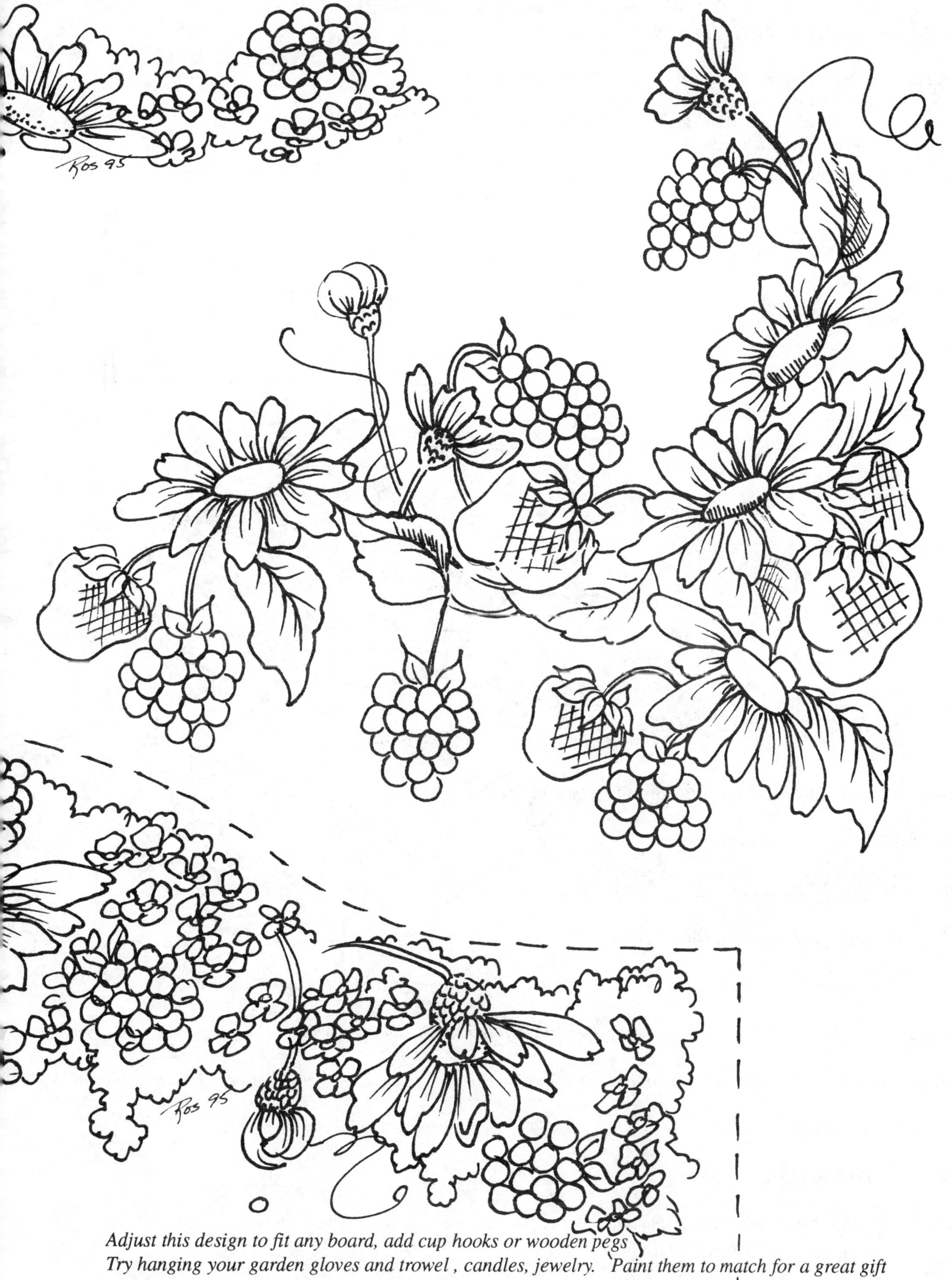

Adjust this design to fit any board, add cup hooks or wooden pegs
Try hanging your garden gloves and trowel , candles, jewelry. Paint them to match for a great gift

Huckleberries and Bows

Repeat parts of this design on a wooden frame and have mirror cut to fit

How about a simple shelf or small chest. Bet you all have some great treasures just waiting to be turned into heirlooms.

Curved wooden box avaliable from Stan Brown's Arts and Craft

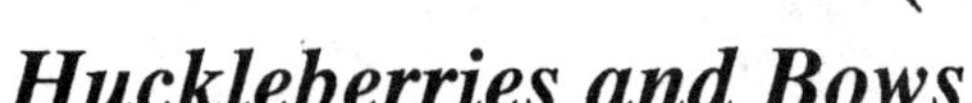

Huckleberries and Bows

Surface: *Curved wooden box. Stan Brown's Arts and Crafts*

Paints: *DecoArt Americana Acrylics*

Basecoat: *J.W. White Lightning*

Foliage: *Avocado, Evergreen, Olive Green*

Daisies: *Titanium White, Paint centers with Cadmium Yellow, shade with Burnt Sienna.*

Ribbons: *Base with Baby Blue. Shade with Blue and highlight with Titanium White.*

Huckleberries: *Q-Tip with Dioxazine Purple and Titanium White.*

Squiggles and Stems: *Avocado.*

Spatter: *Glorious Gold*

Edge box with wash of Brush and Blend and color of your choice.

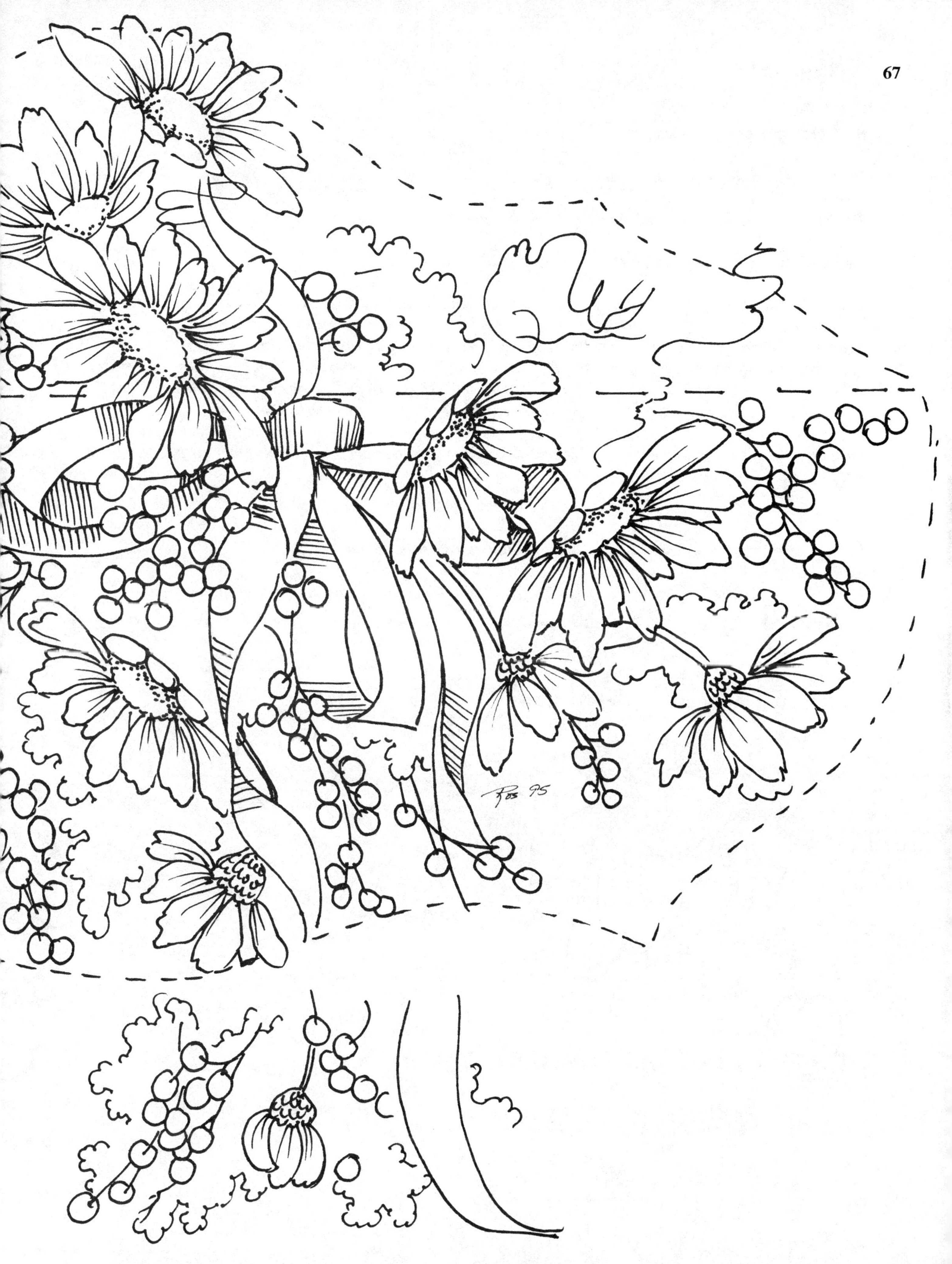
Ros 95

Grape Vines

Surface: *Dark Green Sweatshirt*

Paints: *DecoArt So Soft Fabric Paint*

For best results always pre-wash fabric. No fabric softener

Foliage: *Avocado. Cadmium Yellow, Bright Green and Turquoise*

Transfer Pattern: *Leaves and Grapes. Tulle Method using white Chalk Pencil*

Leaves: *Do not base leaves with any color. Use Angle Shader or Flat Brush, stand brush vertical placing chisel edge of the brush on the edge of the leaf and pull with a lifting motion toward stem end. Vary colors using Avocado with Cadmium Yellow and White or Turquoise and White. Highlight one edge of leaf and a curved line down the center. Highlight the other edge. Allow shirt color to be your darkest value.*

Grapes: *Base with Dioxazine Purple. Shade with Cranberry Wine, True Blue, and Raspberry Pink. Highlight with Turquoise, Baby Blue, White.*

Stems: *Dark Chocolate and White.*

Squiggles: *Avocado Green*

Always follow paint manufactures washing instructions.

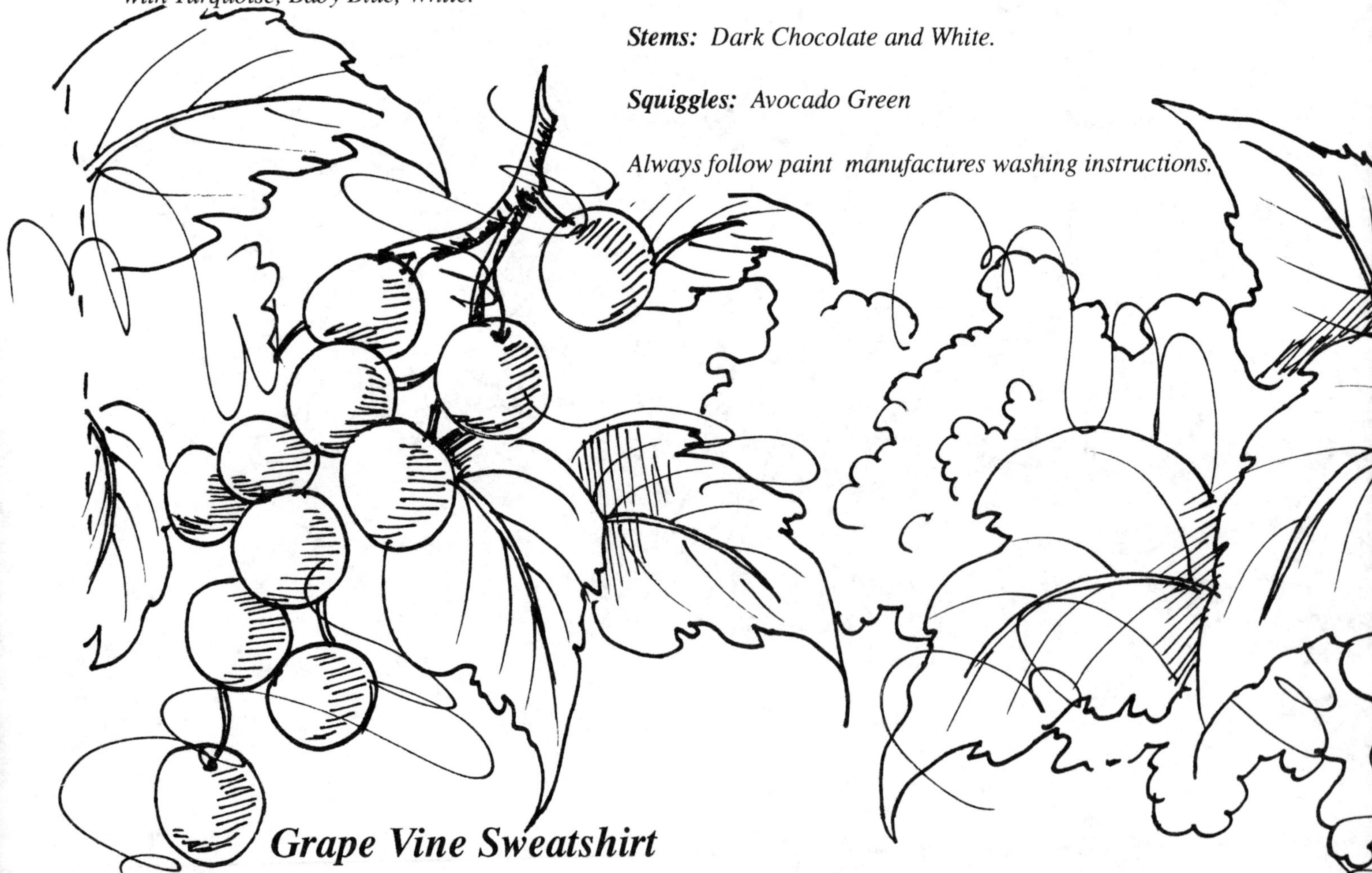

Grape Vine Sweatshirt

Slip shirt onto oval neck board. *Repeat design for back of shirt.*
Coordinate with matching tote bag and canvas shoes.

Try using parts of this design on place mats and napkins.

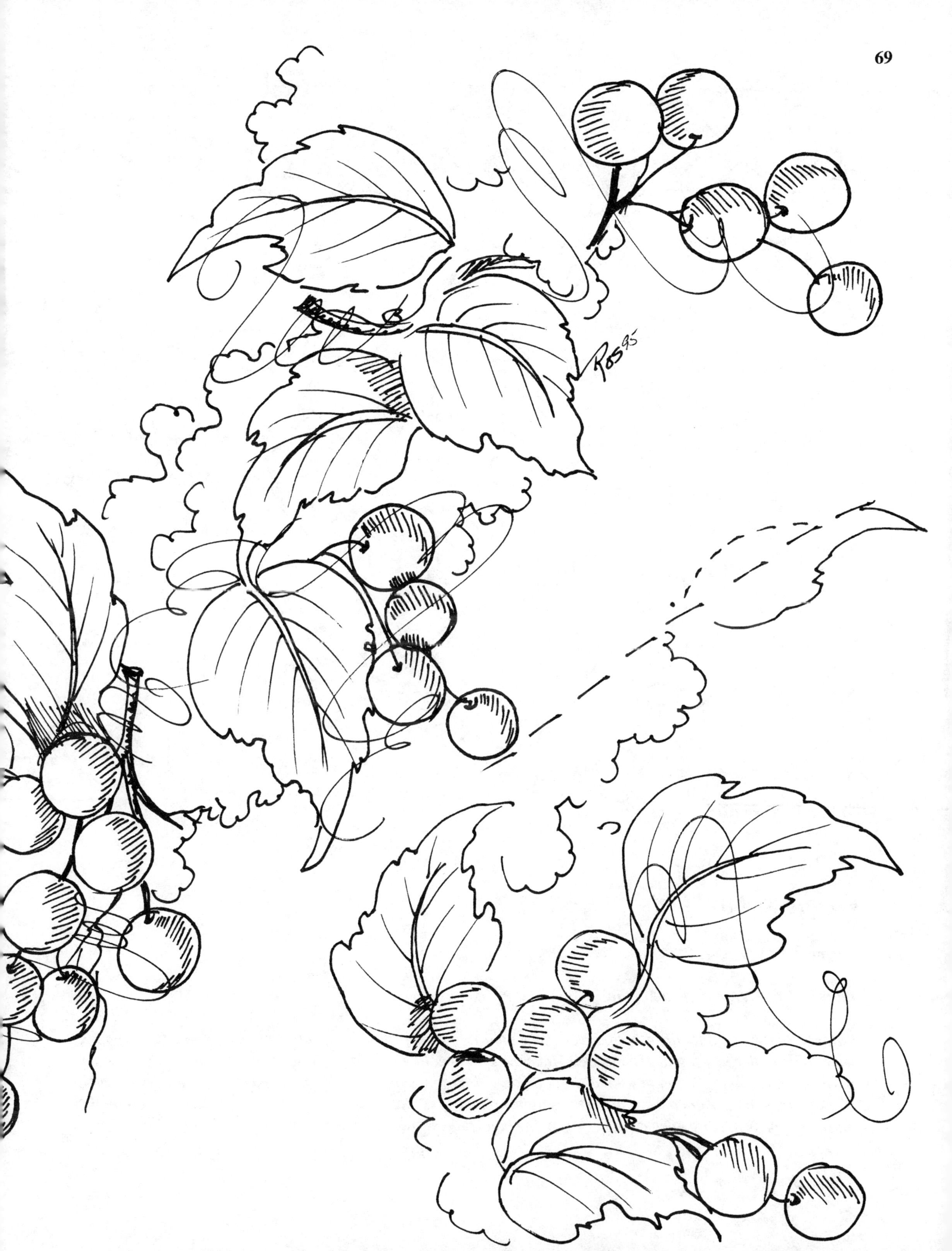
Ros95

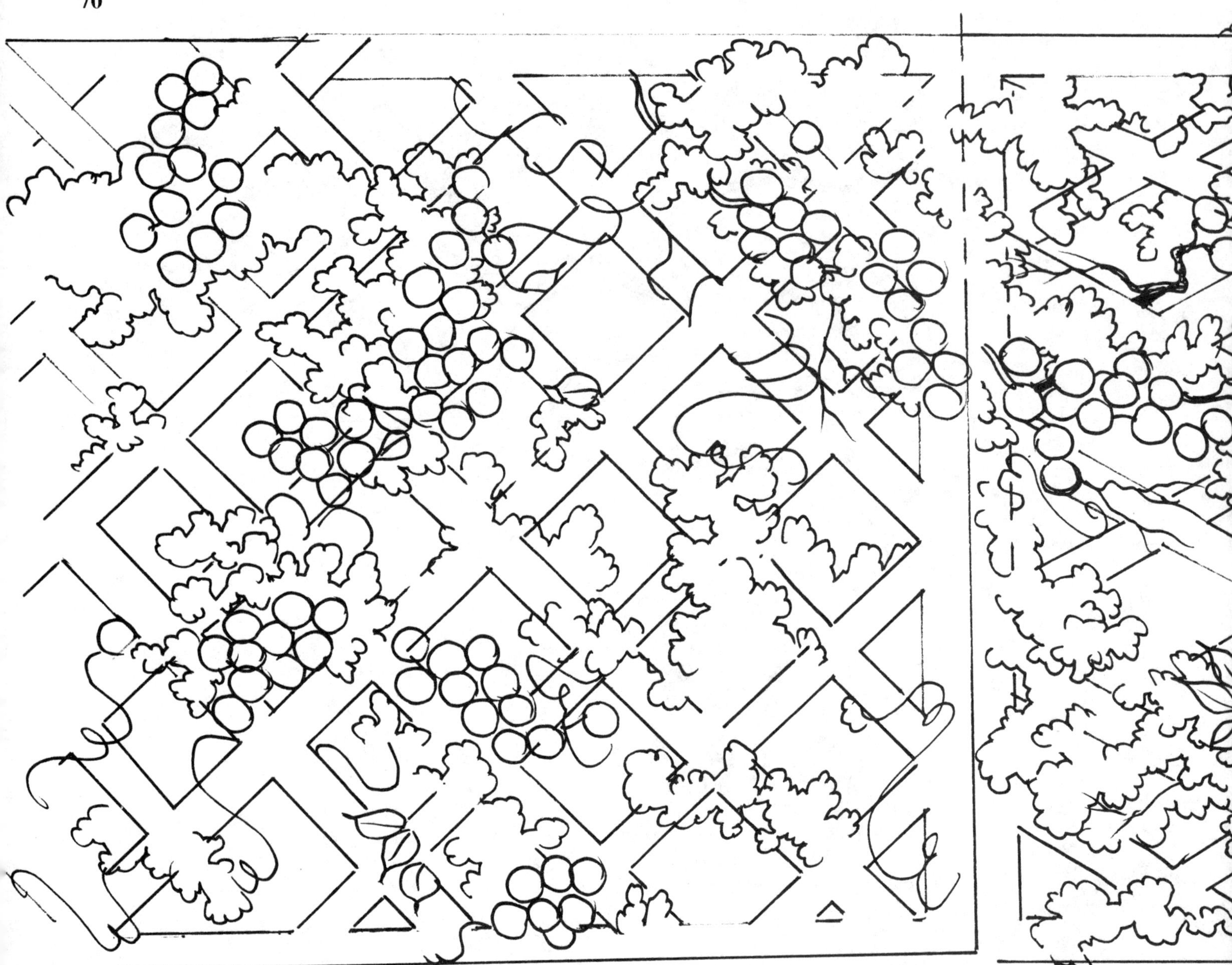

Grape Arbor

Surface: *Box to cover 2 liter or 5 liter box of wine*

Paint: *DecoArt Americana Acrylic*

Lattice: *Draw diagonal lines, both directions, with a ruler and pencil across all surfaces of the box I used the width of my ruler as my unit of measure. Make the first line diagonal from corner to corner and make all lines parallel. Draw one section at a time, do not worry if the lines do not meet at the edges. Tape with 1/4 inch masking tape to the right of each pencil line. Tape up all edges and around the arch on each side. Make sure the masking tape is making good contact by running your fingers over the tape.*

Grape Arbor

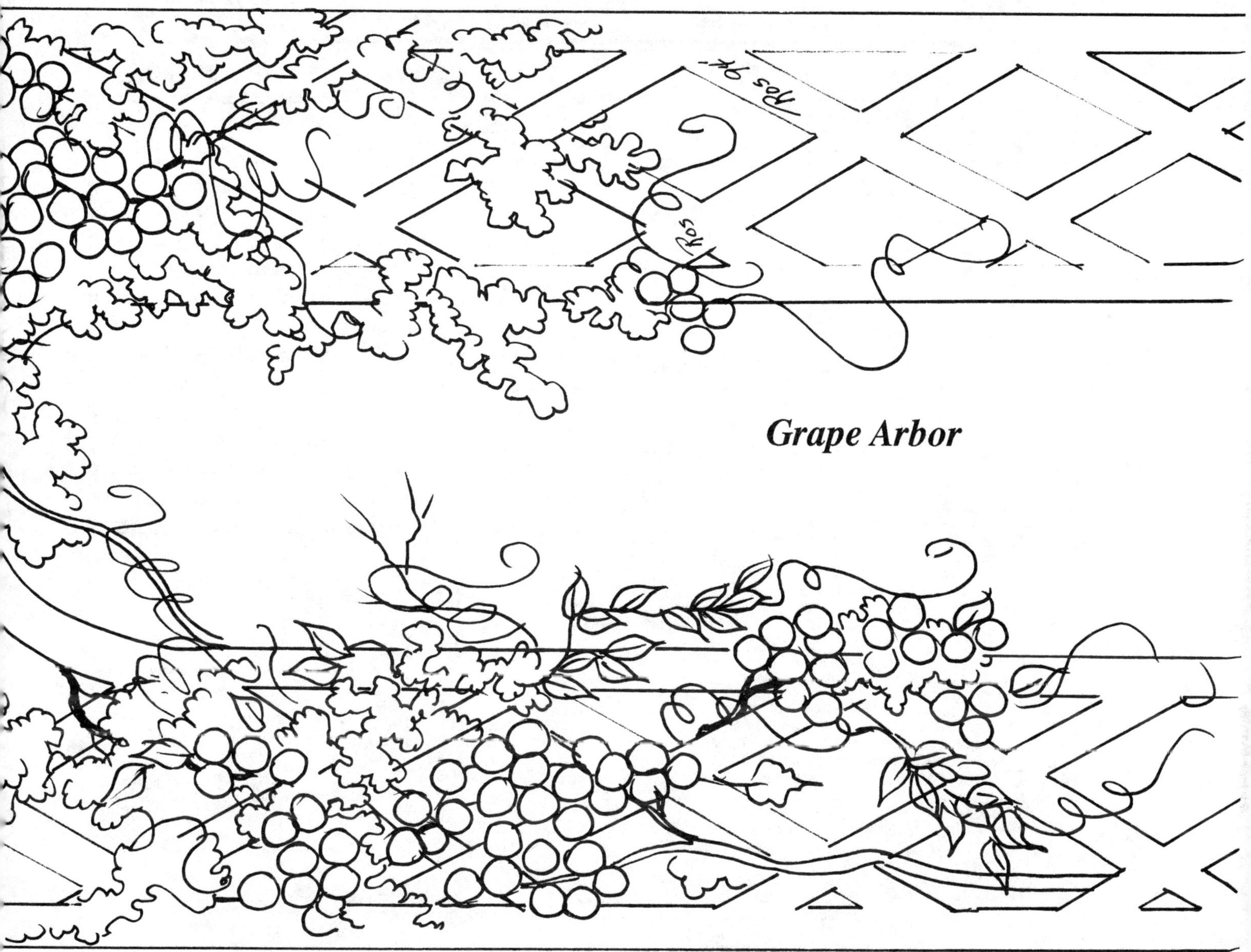

Repeat on other sides

Background Foliage and Grass: *Flip up grass with Olive Green and Mint Julep. Tap foliage with Baby Blue, Olive Green, Mint Julep and Avocado. Allow to dry and remove masking tape. Erase any pencil lines with a soft eraser. Tap foliage on top of the lattice arbor with Evergreen and Dioxazine Purple.*

Grapes: *Pattern bunches of grapes with gray graphite as desired. Paint grapes as little ovals with Lavender and Burgundy Wine Shade on the right side with Dioxazine Purple, Baby Blueand True Blue. Highlight with Orchid, Lavender, and Titanium White.*

Vines & Tendrils: *Dark Chocolate and Dark Chocolate with White*

Susan Scheewe Publications, Inc.

ACRYLIC BOOKS

	Vol.	Title	No.	Price
	Vol. 19	"Gift of Painting" by Susan Scheewe	230	$9.50____
	Vol. 1	"Painting It's Our Bag" by Bev Hink/Susan Scheewe	193	$9.50____
	Vol. 4	"Keepsake Sampler" by Susan & Camille Scheewe	200	$9.50____
	Vol. 1	"Loving You" by Susan & Camille Scheewe	244	$9.50____
	Vol. 1	"Keepsakes For The Holidays" by Charleen Stempel & Susan Scheewe	286	$9.50____
	Vol. 1	"Mrs. MacGregor's Garden" by Charleen Stempel & Susan Scheewe	316	$9.50____
*NEW	Vol. 1	"Country Heartworks" by Reed Baxter	352	$9.50____
	Vol. 1	"Kids And Water" by Joyce Benner	234	$9.50____
	Vol. 2	"The Flower Market" by Joyce Benner	319	$9.50____
	Vol. 1	"Country Fixin's" by Rhonda Caldwell	307	$9.50____
	Vol. 2	"Country Fixin's - Sunflower Friends" by Rhonda Caldwell	321	$9.50____
	Vol. 3	"Country Fixin's - For All Seasons" by Rhonda Caldwell	332	$9.50____
*NEW	Vol. 1	"A Painters Garden" by Jane Dillon	354	$9.50____
	Vol. 1	"Santas and Sams" by Bobi Dolara	258	$9.50____
	Vol. 2	"Vintage Peace" by Bobi Dolara	270	$9.50____
	Vol. 1	"Floral Designs" by Carol Empet	312	$9.50____
	Vol. 2	"Floral Designs 2" by Carol Empet	338	$9.50____
	Vol. 1	"Romantically Tole Bauernmalerei" by Sherry Gall	311	$9.50____
	Vol. 1	"Holiday Gathering" by Angie Hupp	267	$9.50____
	Vol. 3	"Heavenly Gathering" by Angie Hupp	320	$9.50____
	Vol. 1	"Happy Heart, Happy Home" by Cathy Jones	241	$9.50____
	Vol. 1	"Pickets & Pastimes" by Marie & Jim King	329	$9.50____
*NEW	Vol. 2	"Pickets & Pastimes 2, Heart of The Seasons" by Marie & Jim King	348	$9.50____
	Vol. 1	"Huckleberry Horse" by Hanna Long	269	$9.50____
	Vol. 2	"Love Lives Here" by Mary Lynn Lewis	185	$6.50____
	Vol. 3	"Love Lives Here" by Mary Lynn Lewis	195	$6.50____
	Vol. 1	"Special Welcomes" by Corinne Miller	287	$9.50____
	Vol. 2	"Special Welcomes" by Corinne Miller	298	$9.50____
	Vol. 3	"Special Welcomes #3, Crazy About Crafting" by Corinne Miller	309	$9.50____
	Vol. 4	"Special Welcomes #4 Farm-N-Friends" by Corinne Miller	324	$9.50____
	Vol. 5	"Special Welcomes #5 All Wrapped Up" by Corinne Miller	333	$9.50____
*NEW	Vol. 6	"Special Welcomes #6 Crop Keepers" by Corinne Miller	347	$9.50____
	Vol. 1	"Change With The Seasons, Wire Loops" by Joanna Miller	331	$9.50____
	Vol. 1	"Fruit & Flower Fantasies" by Joyce Morrison	277	$9.50____
	Vol. 1	"Wildflower Sampler" by Bev Norman	191	$9.50____
	Vol. 1	"Whimsical Critters" by Lori Ohlson	228	$7.50____
	Vol. 2	"Sunflower Farm" by Lori Ohlson	326	$9.50____
	Vol. 1	"Holiday Medley" by Nina Owens	265	$9.50____
	Vol. 2	"Another Holiday Medley" by Nina Owens	296	$9.50____
	Vol. 1	"Oh Those Little Rascals" by Diane Permenter	247	$9.50____
	Vol. 6	"Acrylic Charms" by Sharon Rachal	305	$9.50____
	Vol. 1	"Forever In My Heart" by Diane Richards.....AC/Fabric	188	$6.50____
	Vol. 2	"Memories In My Heart" by Diane Richards.....AC/Fabric	189	$6.50____
	Vol. 3	"Forever In My Heart II" by Diane Richards.....AC/Fabric	205	$9.50____
	Vol. 6	"Angels In My Stocking" by Diane Richards	254	$9.50____
	Vol. 7	"Nostalgic Dreams" by Diane Richards	273	$9.50____
*NEW	Vol. 8	"Angel Kisses" by Diane Richards	346	$9.50____
	Vol. 1	"Holiday Hangarounds" by Marsha Sellers	327	$9.50____
	Vol. 1	"Creations In Canvas...and More" by Carol Spooner	256	$9.50____
	Vol. 1	"Gran's Garden" by Ros Stallcup	295	$9.50____
	Vol. 2	"Another Gran's Garden" by Ros Stallcup	315	$9.50____
	Vol. 3	"Gran's Garden & House" by Ros Stallcup	334	$9.50____
*NEW	Vol. 4	"Gran's Garden Party" by Ros Stallcup	345	$9.50____
	Vol. 1	"Christmas Greetings from the Cottage" by Chris Stokes	336	$9.50____
	Vol. 1	"Christmas Visions" by Max Terry	285	$9.50____
	Vol. 3	"Painting Clay Pot-pourri" by Max Terry	310	$9.50____
	Vol. 1	"Country Primitives" by Maxine Thomas	274	$9.50____
	Vol. 2	"Country Primitives 2" by Maxine Thomas	300	$9.50____
	Vol. 3	"Country Primitives 3" by Maxine Thomas	322	$9.50____
*NEW	Vol. 4	"Country Primitives 4" by Maxine Thomas	350	$9.50____
	Vol. 1	"Rise & Shine" by Jolene Thompson	214	$6.50____
	Vol. 2	"Garden Gate" by Jolene Thompson	250	$9.50____
	Vol. 5	"Count Your Blessings" by Chris Thornton	213	$9.50____
	Vol. 6	"Share Your Blessings" by Chris Thornton	226	$9.50____
	Vol. 7	"Blessings" by Chris Thornton	255	$9.50____
	Vol. 8	"Christmas Blessings" by Chris Thornton	266	$9.50____
	Vol. 9	"Blessings For The Home" by Chris Thornton	275	$9.50____
	Vol. 10	"Bazaar Blessings" by Chris Thornton	299	$9.50____
	Vol. 11	"Painted Blessings" by Chris Thornton	323	$9.50____
*NEW	Vol. 12	"Family Blessings" by Chris Thornton	349	$9.50____
*NEW	Vol. 13	"Summer Blessings" by Chris Thornton	356	$9.50____
	Vol. 1	"Watermelon Wedges and Rustic Edges" by Lorinne Thurlow	342	$9.50____
*NEW	Vol. 2	"Watermelon Wedges and Rustic Edges 2" by Lorinne Thurlow	353	$9.50____
	Vol. 1	"Barnyard Friends" by Lou Ann Trice	306	$9.50____
	Vol. 5	"Daydreams & Sweet Shirts II" by Don & Lynn Weed	208	$9.50____
	Vol. 1	"Connie's Favorite Old-Time Labels" by Connie Williams	335	$9.50____
*NEW	Vol. 2	"Connie's Garden Seed Packets" by Connie Williams	351	$9.50____
	Vol. 1	"Floral Fabrics and Watercolor" by Sally Williams	262	$9.50____
	Vol. 1	"A Time For Giving" by Evelyn Wright	308	$9.50____

****

SHIPPING & HANDLING CHARGES

Add $2.50 for the First Book for shipping and handling.

Add $1.50 per each additional book.

Please Add $3.00 for handling & postage. PER TAPES. Sorry we must have a "NO REFUND - NO RETURN" policy.

U.S CURRENCY

VISA MasterCard

PRICES SUBJECT TO CHANGE WITHOUT NOTICE

FOR MORE INFORMATION ON BOOKS OR SUPPLIES CALL OR WRITE US

WE ARE ALWAYS GLAD TO HEAR FROM YOU!

5-14-96

13435 N.E. Whitaker Way Portland, Or. 97230 PH(503)254-9100 FAX(503)252-9508

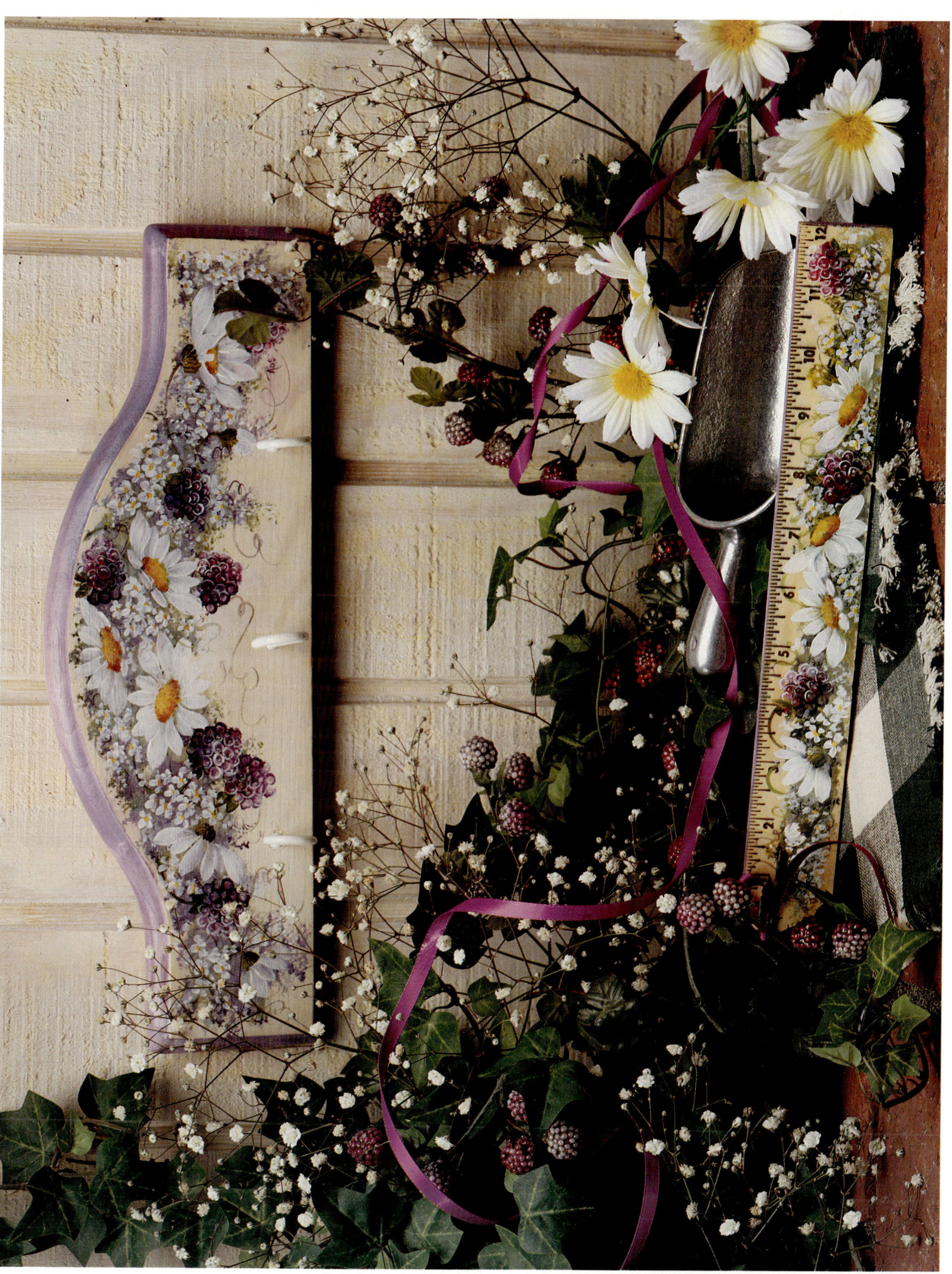

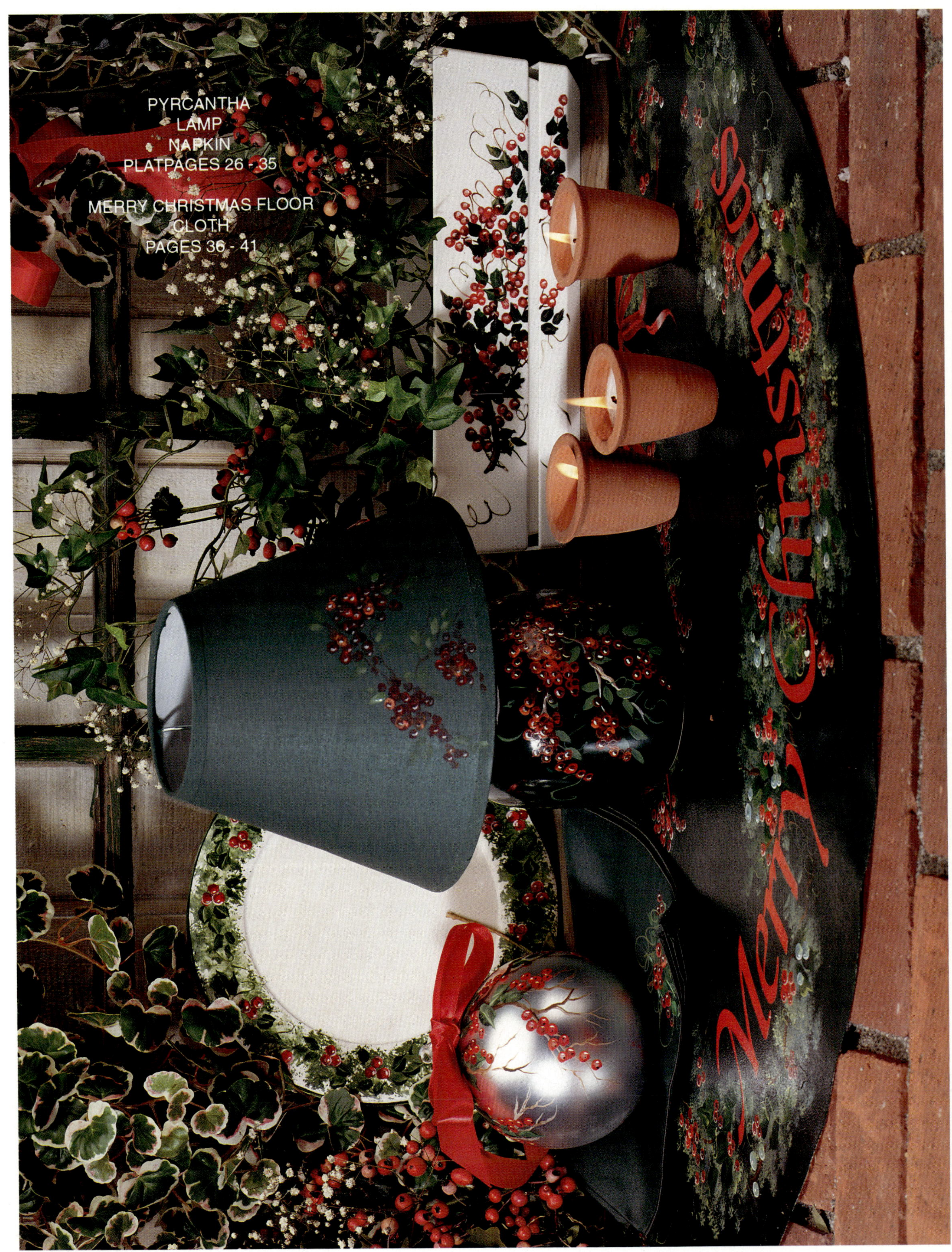

PYRCANTHA
LAMP
NAPKIN
PLATPAGES 26 - 35

MERRY CHRISTMAS FLOOR
CLOTH
PAGES 36 - 41